The Medieval Drama

Contributors

Omer Jodogne
University of Louvain, Belgium

Wolfgang Michael
University of Texas at Austin

Sandro Sticca
State University of New York at Binghamton

V. A. Kolve
University of Virginia

Glynne Wickham
University of Bristol, **England**

William L. Smoldon
Essex, England

THE
MEDIEVAL
DRAMA

Papers of the third annual conference
of the Center for Medieval and
Early Renaissance Studies
State University of New York at Binghamton
3 - 4 May 1969

EDITED BY SANDRO STICCA

State University of New York Press

Albany

First published in 1972 by
State University of New York Press
99 Washington Avenue, Albany, New York 12210

Second printing, 1973

Library of Congress Cataloging in Publication Data

The medieval drama.
"Papers of the third annual conference of the Center for Medieval
and Early Renaissance Studies, State University of New York at
Binghamton, 3–4 May 1969."
English or French.
Includes bibliographies.
1. Drama, Medieval—Congresses. I. Sticca, Sandro, 1931–   ed.
II. New York (State). State University at Binghamton.
Center for Medieval and Early Renaissance Studies.
PN1751.M4 1972   809'.2'02   78–152517
ISBN 0–87395–085–2
ISBN 0–87395–185–9 (microfiche)

CONTENTS

PREFACE

RESEARCH on the complex and vast literary production of the Middle Ages does not permit us to reconstruct with exactness the history of all its genres, the drama, in particular. But the available texts allow us to consider as certainty what some scholars have traditionally regarded as assumptions: the non-existence during the entire Middle Ages of an authentic secular theater either as survival or imitation of the classical one (bearing in mind the true significance of theater, which requires scenic action actually performed by actors impersonating the characters with voice and gestures), and the birth *de novo* of modern drama from the liturgy of the Church. The inferior modes of representation of the mime and panto-mime, the limited and undramatic notions of comedy and tragedy possessed by the Middle Ages, and its meager and blurred understanding of the formal drama in the ancient world, suggest the absence during the Middle Ages of a secular dramatic tradition.

To be sure, the histrionic tradition persisted in a multiplicity of forms, the more widely disseminated being that of the mime. It is now generally agreed that the performance of the mimes differed considerably from the modern theatrical production. Already during the Empire the old *histrio* (actor) had been supplanted by the *pantomimus*, and by the fifth and sixth centuries they came to be associated with the *mimus*, whose repertory consisted of a facile and clever imitation of human customs and lewd scenes in which panderers, prostitutes, and adulterers were portrayed. Such, too, appears to be the medieval application of these terms, as indicated in Papias' "Mimus... id est ioculator et proprie rerum humanarum imitator sicut olim erant in recitatione comediarum quia, quod verbo recitator dicebat, mimi motu corporis exprimebant,"[1] and Isidore's "Histriones sunt qui muliebri indumento gestus impudicarum feminarum exprimebant, hi autem saltando etiam historias et res gestas exprimebant."[2] Concerned in his work with transmitted knowledge and its sources, Isidore is here referring to past practices, as evidenced by the tense used. To be sure, he must have known contemporary *mimi* and *histriones* who gave imitation of "human things" or stories. But one ought to distinguish, as Allardyce Nicoll does, between acting in the old classic tradition of mimic impersonation with its "imitation" of life, and ancient, or for that matter modern, dramatic performance utilizing actors, dialogue, and action.

The survival of the mimes' inferior modes of performance cannot be questioned, particularly in view of the frequent anathemas pronounced against them by the Church. Since we lack, however, all records of dramatic performance between the fifth and the ninth centuries, we need not assume, as some scholars have, that the *mimi* and *histriones* served to keep alive the traditions of the ancient Roman theater until the appearance of the religious drama of the Middle Ages, nor that they were the *causa causans* of this theater. They simply attested the survival of some kind of histrionic instinct, possessing within definite limitations what Fergusson calls "histrionic sensibility."[3]

The true origin of modern drama must be found in the development of the medieval theater, which is a creation of the Church. Action, impersonation, and dialogue, the *sine qua non* of drama, appear in the Roman liturgy, which provided during the liturgical year all kinds of antiphonal responses between a cantor and the Chorus, or between two alternating Choruses. In addition, a general analysis of fundamental Christian theological themes, particularly Christ's passion, will reveal that the Church possesses in the sacred liturgy a dramatic potentiality and intensity of the highest degree.

The intense dramatic feeling noted in the liturgy of the ninth and tenth centuries, the period when religious drama is supposed to have originated, is already present in the rituals of the early Christian Church. Among the most ancient works describing the ritual of its *officia* is the *Aetheriae peregrinatio ad loca sancta*, first discovered and published by Gamurrini in 1887,[4] attributed to St. Sylvia of Aquitaine, sister of Rufinus, and now reputed to have been written at Constantinople by a Galician nun named Etheria between 381 and 395.[5] The second is a *Lectionarius Armenianus* probably composed during the years 464-468;[6] the third, the *Kanonarion* of the Church of Jerusalem dated not earlier than 634-638.[7] The fourth is the *Typicon* (ordo) of the Church of Jerusalem, preserved in a manuscript of the twelfth century but written between the ninth and tenth centuries.[8] These are of considerable interest as sources of information in the study of liturgical offices, but by far the most important is the *Peregrinatio*, for it treats at length the rites of Holy Week of the Church of Jerusalem, the disposition of the canonical hours, the role of the clergy in the various ceremonies, and it contains a most vivid description of the procession to the holy places associated with Christ's Passion.[9] The *Peregrinatio*, transcribed in Cassino in the eleventh century by Petrus Diaconus at the order of the abbot Desiderius (1057-1086), who later became Pope Victor III,[10] has been unduly neglected by medievalists. Recent studies, particularly those of Bastiaensen and Pétré,[11] have shed much light on it.

The germinal point of religious drama is not, however, to be found in the liturgy but in the trope. The trope is usually defined as a verbal amplification of a passage in the authorized liturgy—an introduction, interpolation, addition, or conclusion or a combination of these. Originally, *tropos* was a musical term for a short cadence or melisma added to a syllabic melody. Later it referred to a purely textual addition to a chant or a new composition combining a new text with a new melody. The custom arose during the eighth and ninth century of frequently troping the *Introitus*, the *Kyrie* and the *Gloria*.

The most important trope for the history of modern drama,

however, was the *Quem quaeritis*, which was sung antiphonally before the Introit of the Easter morning Mass and later at the end of Matins. In its most primitive form it is to be found in a manuscript of the tenth century from St. Gall; the oldest extant example, but less primitive in form, was composed between 923 and 924 at the monastery of St. Martial of Limoges. Antiphonally sung at first, the *Quem quaeritis* trope recounted the story of the visit of the Marys to Christ's empty sepulchre, the angelic interrogation, and the Marys' reply. In its rudimentary elaboration of the commemorative ritual, the liturgical action remained void of dramatic significance. Soon, however, it was provided with explicit directions for staging and additional scenes, and by acquiring mimetic action it became an authentic play: the *Visitatio Sepulchri*.

Conclusive and irrefutable evidence has marked the tropes as the essential element that engendered the religious theater, for they exhibit all the ingredients of drama: a definite and visible place of action, impersonation by performers of characters, and use of dialogue. Performed within the confines of Christian worship and subservient to the ends of that worship, they exhibit dramatic action and liturgical rite in the closest conjunction. Spanning many centuries, they are testimony of the growth of the liturgical dramatic form and of the dramatic movement and temper of the liturgy in which they find their origin. An attitude of hostility persists nonetheless in certain scholarly quarters, based on the seeming paradox that the trope came into being at a time when the Church was issuing edicts against the secular stage, and on the assumption that the Church, in general, had been antagonistic toward the theater from the earliest beginnings of the Christian era.

Although the irregular and secular additions to religious drama practiced by some communities, particularly in the eleventh and twelfth centuries, brought about the suspicion of the local episcopal authority and its sanctions, it is a fallacy to assume that the Church as a whole was hostile to the religious stage. The existence of sporadic ecclesiastical injunctions and restrictions did not hinder the development of the religious drama, for the Church in its official legislation of universal pertinence never condemned the religious stage, which flourished with her approval. With spiritual awareness, St. Ethelwold declared that the liturgical drama was to be directed "ad fidem indocti uulgi ac neophytorum corroborandam." As long as primitive drama was motivated by this catechistic and edifying purpose, it remained an integral part of the Church's service, and it flourished with her apparent blessing and approval. The Church fully realized the utility of a religiously inspired dramatic art and did not hesitate to make use of pagan culture as long as it was for the greater glory of God and the edification and salvation of His creatures.

Like the Church which produced it, the medieval drama was international, and from its earliest beginnings in the tenth-century *Quem quaeritis*, to the thirteenth century *Ludi Paschales*, Latin Passion Plays, and the fourteenth and fifteenth century mystery cycles and Passion Plays, its function is quite clear. It constitutes a powerful dramatic statement on the Christian faith at its richest and most complex. The aim of medieval drama is that which motivated the medieval Church as a whole: to express in visible, dramatic terms the facts and values of the accepted body of Scripture and theological belief. Christian art, particularly the dramatic art, is more than a pleasing ornament; it is actually woven into the fabric of Christian thought.

The following six essays, which were read at a conference sponsored by the Center for Medieval and Early Renaissance Studies of the State University of New York at Binghamton on 3-4 May 1969, are contributions toward the examination and elucidations of specific topics and problems concerning the medieval drama. The arresting feature of these essays is their complete independence of each other and their logical movement toward separate conclusions without in any way conflicting with the thematic substance of the general topic. Whatever interaction they may exhibit, it is primarily due to the sacramental and Christian doctrine which shaped the medieval drama and within which the speakers articulated their critical secular perspective.

In "Le théâtre français du moyen âge: Recherches sur l'aspect dramatique des textes", Mr. Jodogne carefully establishes a difference, on the aesthetic level, between the dramatic works and their theatrical performance. He points out that the surviving texts, whether they were meant for reading or a theatrical performance, reproduce only what was said on the stage, and, succinctly, what was done. The text is far from being the whole dramatic work. By imagining the long hours of the performance, one discovers in the manuscripts and in the printed texts numerous characteristics that can be explained, it seems, only by stage requirements and concessions to a demanding public. One grasps first of all the need to create silence and then a religious atmosphere surviving even the performance. To entertain one needs variety, and hence one cogently perceives the necessity of the changes in tone, in metrical schemes, the songs and the melodies.

Mr. Jodogne calls attention to the fact that the sequence and the choice of scenes are dictated both by the subject and by stage requirements. The author has to be guided by theatrical considerations such as the appropriate stage-place for the actors, the necessity to avoid dull stretches by filling the conventional length of a journey, the entertainment of the public by presenting on stage traditional comic characters and by inserting earthy scenes or broad farce in the sacred drama.

While contributing to lengthen the play, to make it less dense or even diffuse, these concessions nevertheless prevent complete unity of tone, even in the case of a sacred tragedy like the Passion. But if one is willing to exercise aesthetic distance, Mr. Jodogne concludes, it is still possible to enjoy the frequent and unexpected variations of these Mysteries which offer a cosmos similar in heterogeneity to mankind.

In his essay on "Tradition and Originality in the Medieval Drama in Germany, " Mr. Michael suggests that the first medieval drama, the *Visitatio Sepulchri* of the *Regularis Concordia* of Winchester (965-75), did not originate in a slow growth from the Easter trope *Quem quaeritis;* it was rather an original creation of the author or authors of the *Concordia*. Although most of the following liturgical dramatic endeavors in their slow process of change and expansion show mainly the working of tradition, Mr. Michael feels that a few pieces betray an original spirit and form. In Germany, for example, the *Tegernsee Antichrist*, although using a tenth century-treatment as its source, handles this material with superior nonchalance. The liveliness in diction and in metric form indicate the brilliant black sheep of the Middle Ages at work, the *clerici vagantes*. The same spirit of superiority, the same freedom of form pervades not only the half dozen later dramas in the famous vagantic collection of the *Carmina Burana*, but also gives many of the following dramas in the vernacular special spice and effect. But in the waning Middle Ages, craftsmen and the patriciate of the growing cities established traditions of performances that left scant or no room for original dramatic creations. Even if the directors of the plays were active dramatists, as for instance Bletz and Salat, the traditional form remained.

In the secular drama in the Fastnachtspiel, Hans Rosenplüt and Hanz Folz enhanced a basically traditional form with traits of originality; but a really original form of this genre was only attained much later by the genius Hans Sachs. Mr. Michael concludes by stating that all the medieval dramas must have gained in a lively originality in the one aspect of which we know least—the performance on stage.

In "The Literary Genesis of the Latin Passion Play and of the *Planctus Mariae*: A New Christocentric and Marian Theology," Mr. Sticca examines the medieval liturgical ceremonies commemorating events in Christ's Passion and traces their gradual change in character from the contemplative to the dramatic.

The author shows that while Christ's passion became increasingly popular as one of the sacred mysteries beginning in the tenth century, new forces that allowed a more eloquent and humane visualization and description of Christ's anguish first appeared in the eleventh and twelfth centuries. He shows how this general shift towards a realistic depiction of the Passion exhibits a preference for emotional rather than intellectual apprehension of dogma, and offers a new theory of the inception of the Latin Passion Play as a literary form developed by the Montecassino monastic circle and influenced by the changing themes in liturgy, art, and literature of the eleventh century. Mr. Sticca concludes the essay by discussing and refuting the traditional view that the *Planctus Mariae* is the germinal point of the Latin Passion Play.

In *"Everyman* and the Parable of the Talents," Mr. Kolve seeks to account for certain central facts about the play that have never had any close critical attention: the hero as a man summoned to render accounts, the journey he is commanded to go, the second set of friends who desert him (Strength, V. Wyttes, Beaute, Dyscrecion), and the sustained ambiguity of pronoun in God's long opening speech, in which Everyman is spoken of as both "he" and "they." Mr. Kolve initiates his critical analysis of the play by examining in close detail the parable of the talents from Matthew 25, for it (along with associated parables concerning talents in Luke 19 and Matthew 18) offers a source from which all these may be said to derive. From these premises he cogently shows how the parable and its associated commentaries offer help in the understanding of other actions and characters as well. He concludes by pointing out the crucial influence in the shaping of *Everyman* of the *Speculum Humanae Salvationis* and of an eleventh-century Greek original of the testing-of-friends story.

The sixth essay concerns itself with drama as a theatrical performance. Mr. Wickham begins his discussion of "The Staging of Saint Plays in England" by cautioning the reader against the fallacies of the evolutionary explanation of dramatic development of Saint Plays in England, and by exploding, after a discussion of the range in nature and quality of English Saint Plays on the evidence of reference alone, the old categorizing of these plays as a by-product or late development of Mysteries and Moralities. He then turns to a critical discussion of the three surviving texts of English Saint Plays—*St. Paul, St. Mary Magdalene* and *St. Meriasek*—and of their original staging, by means of diagrammatic illustrations which provide an integral and vivid visualization of their performance. He concludes his study with a discussion of the aesthetics of one Saint Play, *St. Meriasek*, in its original context and in modern revival. Mr. Wickham points out that the reenactment of this play provided the actors and himself with an insight into the artistic skill, stage craft, and ability to instruct possessed by those anonymous dramatists who created and produced Saint Plays in England.

The last essay, "The Origins of the '*Quem Quaeritis*' Trope and the Easter Sepulchre Music-Dramas, as Demonstrated by their Musical Settings," deals with the relationship between music and drama. Mr. Smoldon approaches on unaccustomed lines the still controversial question of the origins of the *Quem quaeritis* dialogue. Possessing as he does photographs of all the worth-while manuscripts of the liturgical dramas of the medieval Church, which he insists on calling "music-dramas," he has transcribed them all, and from a comparative study of this same music has produced evidence concerning these dramatic works that has not before been realized. He points out that, with a few exceptions, the statements and theories of writers on the subject have been based on the Latin texts alone. Thus, for more than a hundred years, half the possible means of gaining knowledge concerning these dramatic works has been disregarded. He maintains that when musical evidence is called on, it may certainly confirm some statement or theory of a "textual" writer, but on the other hand, on a number of occasions he has found that it brings about a confutation; and that even that great scholar, Karl Young, can be shown to be in error at times. Of particular moment is the case of a recent book, *Christian Rite and Christian Drama in the Middle Ages* by O.B. Hardison, which, Smoldon maintains, can be seen time and again to be at fault through the author's failure to show any appreciation of the *music* of the liturgy of the dramas. Smoldon holds that Hardison's "Vigil Mass" theory concerning the origin of the *Quem quaeritis* dialogue does not survive a consideration of the musical nature of the tropes.

The most important matter of debate concerns the original home of the *Quem quaeritis* trope. Photographs of the two earliest surviving manuscripts of the trope, that from St. Martial of Limoges (*Bibl. Nat. MS lat.* 1240) and that from the Abbey of St. Gall (*St. Gall,* MS 484) were shown on the screen. From a detailed consideration of the trope notation of each of them, and from evidence from the music of other early ones, Smoldon shows himself convinced that the place of origin of the trope was the Abbey of St. Martial of Limoges, even though *MS 1240* may represent only the earliest *surviving* version. As an offshoot of the Limoges arguments, the speaker shows that musical evidence is strong for assuming that the *Quem quaeritis* dialogue music of the Winchester Troper Easter Sepulchre music-drama had travelled from Limoges.

Sandro Sticca

NOTES

1. Gustavo Vinay, "La commedia latina del secolo XII," *Studi Medievali*, 2 (1954), 230.

2. W.M. Lindsay, ed., *Isidori Etymologiae*, 2 vols. (Oxford, 1911), II, Bks. XVIII, XLIX.

3. Francis Fergusson, *The Idea of a Theater* (Garden City, 1953), pp. 251-55.

4. Johannes Franciscus Gamurrini, *S. Hilarii Tractatus de Mysteriis et S. Silviae Aquitanae Peregrinatio ad Loca Sancta* (Rome, 1887).

5. J. B. Thibaut, *Ordre des offices de la Semaine Sainte à Jerusalem du IVe au Xe siècle* (Paris, 1926), p. 8; Hélène Pétré, *Ethérie. Journal de voyage* (Paris, 1948), p. 15.

6. Thibaut, *op. cit.*, p. 9.

7. Ibid., p. 10.

8. Ibid.

9. As Thibaut observes, "ces offices commémoratifs, accomplis sur les Lieux Saints qui furent le théâtre de la douloureuse Passion de Notre-Seigneur, Jésus-Christ, s'étendirent bientôt à toutes les Eglises de la chrétienté, y compris celle de Rome." (Ibid., p. 127). Pope Damasus appears to have introduced this *Ordo* in the Roman liturgy: "Id est primus beatus Damasus papa adjuvante sancto Hieronimi presbytero vel ordinem ecclesiasticum descriptum de Hierosolyma permissu sancti ipsius Damasi transmittentem instituit et ordinavit." (In Martin Gerbert's *Monumenta Veteris Linguae Alemanicae* [Saint-Blasien, 1790], p. 185).

10. D. Mauro Inguanez, "Montecassino e l'Oriente nel Medio-Evo," *Atti del IV Congresso Nazionale di Studi Romani*, 1, (Rome, 1938): 377-84, 380; Harry J. Leon, "A Medieval Nun's Diary," *The Classical Journal*, 59 (1963). 121. Gamurrini, *op. cit.*, ix writes about the *Peregrinatio:* "Sane quidem Petrus Diaconus, qui saeculo duodecimo ineunte post Leonem Marsicanum vel Ostiensem bibliothecarius valde laboriosus in illo floruit coenobio, quum

librum vel Itenerarium—De locis sanctis—confecisset, eamdem Peregrinationem in manus versavit, multa ad verbum prosecutus excepit, atque in sua inserenda curavit." Petrus Diaconus is more widely known as the compiler of Monte-cassino's *De viris illustribus* and for having continued to 1138 the famous *Chronica Casinensis* of Leo of Ostia, who, as the first chronicler, recorded the events of the monastery covering the years 1098 to 1107.

11. A.A.R. Bastiaensen, *Observations sur le vocabulaire liturgique dans l'Itinéraire d'Egérie* (Utrecht, 1962); Hélène Pétré, *Ethérie. Journal de Voyage* (Paris, 1948).

LE THEATRE FRANÇAIS DU MOYEN AGE :
RECHERCHES SUR
L'ASPECT DRAMATIQUE DES TEXTES

Omer Jodogne

APRÈS la représentation théâtrale, le texte n'est plus qu'un reflet partiel de l'œuvre. J'oserais même dire qu'il est plus pauvre avant le jeu qu'après. En effet, le metteur en scène, qui ne serait pas l'auteur, puise dans l'écrit les éléments qui lui permettront de poser ses décors, d'assigner aux acteurs les démarches et le ton qui s'imposent. Très souvent, avant l'exécution de son drame, l'auteur du libretto aura eu le soin de prévoir lui-même, dans des didascalies minutieuses, les accessoires et même les attitudes des exécutants. Si, après la représentation, certains scribes ont pu recopier très exactement le livre en songeant à des représentations futures dans leur ville ou ailleurs, par contre, la plupart des copistes ont dépouillé le libretto des indications scéniques et l'ont transformé tacitement en œuvre à lire.[1]

Par conséquent lorsque nous examinons les textes conservés, nous devons faire un gros effort pour imaginer ce qu'était la représentation elle-même, l'incidence sur les spectateurs de telle réplique, de telle succession de scènes ou de telle interruption à l'intérieur d'un épisode. Car le théâtre est beaucoup plus qu'un texte joué!

Mon intention n'est pas de reconstituer la mise en scène à l'aide des didascalies conservées par certains manuscrits. Elles nous en apprennent beaucoup et on peut rappeler la richesse des indications scéniques du jeu d'*Adam*, des Mystères de la *Résurrection* (Angers 1456; inédit, ms. Chantilly, Condé 615, Paris B.N. fr. 972 et Rés. Yf 15) et de l'*Incarnation* (Rouen 1474).[2] G. Cohen, jadis, a exploité heureusement ces données abondantes et a pu écrire un ouvrage qui est resté classique.[3]

Ce que je voudrais étudier, c'est ce que les textes peuvent nous apprendre de l'ambiance pendant la représentation et des conventions particulières au théâtre. Nous observerons tout d'abord ce qui contribue à créer ou à varier l'atmosphère; puis, nous rechercherons la raison d'être des scènes qui précèdent ou qui interrompent le déroulement de l'action principale. Enfin, nous nous demanderons ce qui, dans le texte, a suscité la réplique de l'interlocuteur.

1. L'appel au silence.

Ce qui paraissait difficile à obtenir lorsqu'un Mystère était représenté sur la place publique, c'était le silence. A Angers, en 1486, le Conseil de la ville a ordonné «que chacun face sillence et obbesisse a ceulx qui sont ordonnez estre au jeu pour faire ladicte sillence...». «Item, et pour mieux commancer et avoir sillence, si l'on voit qu'il soit expediant, sera dicte une messe ou jeu sur ung autel honnestement droissé.»[4]

Et l'appel au silence est fréquent dès les premiers mots d'un drame. Remarquons cette didascalie au début de la Seconde Journée de la *Passion* de Jean Michel:

«Et commencent les apostres faisans une recapitulation des faiz de Jesus traictes en la premiere Journee. Neantmains, la fille de la Chananee pourra commencer la Journee en parlant comme une demoniacle jusques ad ce que bonne silence fust faicte.»

Jean Michel a donc supposé que les spectateurs pourraient ne pas se taire pendant que les apôtres, en 96 vers, résumeraient les événements passés au cours de la Journée précédente. Il a proposé que, dans une tirade (qu'il n'a pas donnée), la fille de la Chananéenne, une démoniaque, vînt s'agiter sur la scène et proférer quelques lazzi qui feraient tendre l'oreille et ramèneraient le silence. Après quoi, les apôtres pourraient parler, assurés d'être entendus.

Même remarque au début de la Tierce Journée: «Et sus l'entree du parc, y aura enfans chantans melodieusement jusques ad ce que bonne silence soit faite, *en lieu de prologue*.» La Quarte Journée commence par un défilé: Anne, Caîphe précédant le Christ, les Pharisiens et les Scribes. Et c'est alors que Judas pourra profiter de l'attention obtenue pour commencer sa longue tirade désespérée (71 vers).

2. Le sermon initial.

En général, c'est un prédicateur qui, parlant le premier en scène, donne le ton à la représentation sur la place publique.

Le *Saint Nicolas* de Jean Bodel commençait *ex abrupto*, et aussi le *Miracle de Théophile*. Mais, quelques dizaines d'années après 1200, pour une nouvelle représentation du drame de Bodel, un anonyme imposa un prologue à dire par le Prêcheur.

La *Passion du Palatinus* ignore ce recours au Prêcheur. Celle du manuscrit Didot renoue avec la tradition, inaugurée semble-t-il, par l'auteur du Prologue du *Saint Nicolas*. On ne sait pas qui parle mais c'est un prêcheur assurément qui se prévaut de l'autorité de Pilate pour recommander le silence et le calme:

> Ouyés, les bons, entendés moy,
> je vous commandes de par le roy,
> de part Pilate le prevost,
> que vous ne disiés ung seult most
> et ne veullés feres moleste... (Version Biard 1-5)

Et c'est non moins plaisamment qu'en fin de tirade il accorde sept ou huit années d'indulgence à ceux qui se tairont:

> Qui se taisera, je ly don
> sep, VIII ans de vray pardon (37-8).

Dans les quarante *Miracles de Nostre Dame par personnages* s'échelonnant de 1346 à 1382, d'auteurs différents, mais travaillant pour la même Confrérie des orfèvres parisiens, 24 pièces seulement commencent par un sermon. Cependant, dans dix d'entre elles, cette allocution du prêcheur n'est insérée qu'après les premières répliques. Par conséquent, le sermon ne remplit plus entièrement le rôle particulier qu'on lui assignait pour amorcer une sorte de cérémonie religieuse. Il faut supposer toutefois que ces Miracles n'étaient pas représentés sur la place publique, mais en salle.

A partir des grands jeux du manuscrit Sainte-Geneviève, la tradition s'établit. C'est un prêcheur qui amorce la pièce par un sermon avec *thème* latin, avec *Ave Maria* sans que soit oublié cet appel au silence:

> Benois soit il qui se tera..
> et fera paix pour mieux oyr...
> (Nativité, éd. R. Whittredge, 1944, vv. 2-3)
> Premierement le sermon:... (Geu des Trois Roys, *Ibid.*)

Ce prêcheur s'appelle *Praedicator* dans chacune des Journées du Mystère de la *Passion de Semur*, *Prescheur* dans la *Passion* d'Arras (et toujours ces recommandations: faictes paix 71, 13288, 18740). Il n'est pas nommé dans le drame de Gréban, celui qui réclame le silence:

> Vueillez vous pour vo salut taire
> par une amoureuse scilence (4-5).
> Si vous prions...
> que scilence vueillez garder (1720-2).
> ...scilence nous vueillez prester (20102).
> ...quoys et paisibles vous rendez (27477).

Marcadé et Gréban, dans leur 2e Journée et Michel, dans la première, ont réussi à substituer saint Jean-Baptiste au prédicateur anonyme.

Le Mystère inédit de la *Résurrection* d'Angers entame chacune de ses trois Journées par un sermon où s'insèrent les appels au calme:

> Mais gardez vous, comme qu'il voise,
> que vous ne facez point de noise,
> car noise peult estre en feroit
> perdre le fruit... (ms Chantilly, 5 vº).
> ...Pour ce, faictes paix et silence (5 vº)
> ...et pense chascun de soy taitre (88 vº).

Le sermon est abandonné dans le Mystère de *l'Incarnation et Nativité* de Rouen (1474). Par contre, un Prologue en 24 vers n'omet pas les recommandations d'usage:

> Nous vous prions tous qu'il vous plaise taire (I, p. 3).
> Si prions de pensee incline
> a chascun que noyse on desine
> et paix ayon a suffisance... (II, p. 1).

3. *Le Te Deum final.*

Une tradition très stable à travers les trois grands siècles du théâtre, consiste à terminer l'œuvre par une action de grâces à Dieu, une hymne de gratitude pour les faits glorieux qu'on lui doit.

Dès le *Saint Nicolas*, nous entendons cette réplique finale:

> A Dieu dont devons nous canter
> hui mais: Te Deum laudamus (1532-3).

Et Rutebeuf de même:

> Chantons tuit por coste novele:
> Or, levez sus;
> Disons: Te Deum laudamus (éd. Grace Frank, 661-2).

Ce ne sont pas les derniers mots de la *Passion du Palatinus*. En effet, le dernier acteur qui parle est Marie-Madeleine qui, sans transition avec ce qui précède, entonne

> Te Deum laudamus,
> te, Domine, confitemur.
> Or deprions a Jhesucrist
> qui pour nous se leissa mourir,
> que il nous doint tele choze faire
> qui a son douz cors puisse plaire,
> et en tiex euvres maintenir
> par quoy nous puissons touz venir
> laissus en paradis tout droit!
> Dites Amen, que Diex l'ottroit! (éd. Grace Frank, 1987-96).

Tout autre chose dans la *Passion Didot* (version Biard). Pas de *Te Deum* ni de salut souhaité aux auditeurs, mais une allocution de Jésus aux pécheurs sur le thème: «Toi qui passe, vois donc s'il est une douleur comparable à la mienne.»

L'auteur de la *Nativité* et du *Jeu des Trois Rois* du manuscrit Sainte-Geneviève s'en tient à cette formule mi-plaisante mi-religieuse:

Sy chantons, *becus et camus*,
chascun: Te Deum laudamus (1195-6)

(et 1561-2, avec cette variante *tant becus que camus* qui allonge le vers d'une syllabe).

La *Résurrection*, qui est peut-être du même auteur, se termine par cette exhortation de Madeleine:

Et vous prie que pour l'excellance
de sa loenge, sanz cillance,
nous esmovons sans tarder plus,
chantant: Te Deum laudamus. (éd. James F. Burks, 1957).

La *Passion* du même manuscrit, due à un auteur différent de celui des trois autres pièces, finit par l'espoir du salut commun exprimé par le Centurion qui poursuit ainsi:

Sy vous diray que nous ferons:
tuit a une vois chanterons
de cuer: Te Deum laudamus
et puis le Benedicamus. Amen.

Cette antienne *Benedicamus* nous prouve qu'on chantait le *Te Deum* entièrement et qu'on ajoutait les versets et les répons.

La *Passion* de Semur fait dire à Jésus, à la fin de la seconde et dernière Journée seulement:

Chantons: Te Deum laudamus (9582).

La tradition semble perdue à Arras, au début du XVe siècle, car Marcadé, à la fin de son Mystère, ne songe plus qu'à souhaiter le salut éternel des spectateur: il abandonne le *Te Deum*, se contentant de cette évocation rituelle de Dieu.

qui est et regne en trinité
et toujours sans fin regnera
in seculorum secula. Amen. (24942-4).

Arnoul Gréban retrouve les usages d'autrefois, mais sans plus penser à la sanctification du public:

6

rendons graces a Dieu le Pere,
chantans Te Deum laudamus. (34428-9).

C'est de la même manière que la *Résurrection* d'Angers (1456) s'achève, mais ce qui lui est particulier, c'est que le chant n'est pas entamé par l'un des acteurs. Une didascalie finale nous renseigne: «Icy fine le mistere et se departent les joueurs pour eulx en aller, chantans ensemble *Te Deum laudamus, te Dominum confitemur*, etc.»

Par contre, l'*Incarnation et Nativité* de Rouen (1474), où les chants abondent, termine très prosaïquement la représentation:

> ...Et loés la grant majesté
> de cil dont la nativité
> est aucunement demonstree! (**II, p. 471**).

Jean Michel termine pieusement ses deux premières Journées, n'oubliant pas de souhaiter le ciel aux assistants. A la fin du drame, celui qui dit le Prologue («allocution») *final*, ne dit pas autre chose que:

> ...la passion de Jesucrist
> ayons en recordacion
> affin que, par compassion,
> puissons meriter mesouen
> et en fin avoir gloire. Amen. (29922-6).

Il omet le *Te Deum*. L'a-t-il oublié? Je ne le crois pas: l'auteur, laissant le Christ dans le tombeau, n'a pas cru séant de chanter l'hymne qui est à la fois un hommage et une manifestation de la joie.

Ainsi donc,—les exemples de Marcadé et de l'*Incarnation* sont probants,—la finale traditionelle est négligée par certains grands auteurs de XVe siècle. Et pourtant, cette hymne très longue, chantée intégralement par les acteurs et par la foule qui se dispersait, était, semble-t-il, le meilleur moyen d'éviter un brouhaha discordant et, d'autre part, d'entretenir les partants dans cette atmosphère de componction voulue par les auteurs.

Nous savons que ce chant final est primitivement celui qui clôturait l'office de Matines, à l'époque où les drames liturgiques étaient exécutés le matin. Dès le *Saint Nicolas* de Jean Bodel, vers

1200 donc, il s'est imposé, semble-t-il, comme fin rituelle d'un drame religieux. Mais, nous le trouvons aussi dans *Courtois d'Arras*, qui est une laïcisation de la parabole de l'Enfant Prodigue. En effet, le père de Courtois n'est pas assimilé à Dieu; au contraire de lui, il ne va pas à sa rencontre et feint même de ne pas le reconnaître. Et nous relevons pourtant cette finale:

> Bien en devons tuer no buef
> de joie k'il est revenus.
> Chantons Te Deum laudamus. (éd. Edmond Faral, 650-2).

Il n'est pas interdit de chanter le *Te Deum* à l'occasion d'un bonheur très profane; mais, tout de même, aucun autre auteur de drame non religieux ne s'est autorisé à finir ainsi la représentation de sa pièce.

Sur ce point aussi, les Miracles du XIVe siècle diffèrent des Mystères. A Paris, 37 *Miracles de Nostre Dame* ont une finale musicale, mais trois se terminent par une simple réplique parlée (V, XXV, XX; les nos XVII et XXXVIII sont inachevés). Plutôt qu'n chant, c'est la musique instrumentale des ménestrels qui ponctue le départ des acteurs (nos XXXI, XXXII, XXXVII). Seul le nº XXXVII préfère le *Te Deum*.

4. La musique.

Cette évocation du *Te Deum* ou de l'hymne finale m'amène à la question de la musique au théâtre: chant et accompagnement instrumental.

Un excellent article de W. Noomen sur le *Jeu d'Adam*[5] nous a prouvé que «le matériel liturgique contenu dans la pièce en détermine la structure fondamentale...», les parties en langue vulgaire n'ayant comme fonction que d'expliciter et d'illustrer cette thématique fondamentale de l'office de la Septuagésime, en l'amplifiant et en y ajoutant des éléments exégétiques. Et nous en arrivons à mieux imaginer ce qu'était le drame: non seulement les textes latins y sont l'essentiel, mais ils sont chantés au complet, alors que le manuscrit ne nous en donne que les premiers mots ou le premier verset. Il faut imaginer que la durée de la représentation était occupée plus que pour moitié par le chant, infiniment plus lent que la parole en langue vulgaire. Ainsi donc, notre perspective change : ce que nous considérions comme une armature ou même comme des gloses scripturaires est en réalité ce que les assistants ont entendu le plus longtemps. Le drame est plus musical que parlé, la parole n'étant que le commentaire du chant, dite bien plus rapidement.

Vers la même époque, la *Résurrection du Sauveur* révèle une conception nouvelle : le chant et la musique sont abandonnés. semble-t-il, à moins que le scribe n'ait négligé les didascalies du libretto.

Pas la moindre musique dans les pièces du XIIIᵉ siècle, *Saint Nicolas*, *Théophile*, *Courtois d'Arras*. Mais une chanson des fées dans le *Jeu de la Feuillée* (éd. Langlois, 874-5) et, on le sait, le *Jeu de Robin et Marion* d'Adam de la Halle est, comme le dit Langlois, «le premier opéra-comique français : le genre, une pastorale dramatique, imposait cette formule mixte.»

Au XIVᵉ siècle, la musique réintègre le théâtre religieux, humblement je l'avoue. Le *Palatinus* fait chanter un enfant lors de l'entrée du Christ à Jérusalem (55-9) et les âmes des Limbes à la descente du Ressuscité (1429—Voir le v. 1426) ; ajoutons-y le *Te Deum* final. C'est peu de chose, mais, à vrai dire, la tragédie de la Passion ne fait aucune place à des chants religieux. La *Passion d'Autun* attribue à Longin une citation chantée de David (version Biard, 1128-39) ; dans l'épisode correspondant, la version Romans fait chanter à Longin et à son compagnon, ce qu'ils veulent (697-8).

Avec les *Miracles de Nostre Dame* s'introduit au théâtre le rondeau et, dans ce répertoire de la Confrérie des orfèvres parisiens, on ne connaît que le rondeau chanté. Il accompagne la descente et la remontée des personnages célestes et il est exécuté par des anges. Aucun Miracle ne manque de rondeaux et tels d'entre eux, les nᵒˢ V (Nativité Nostre Seigneur) et XXX (*Saint Jehan le Paulu*). qui se terminent sans hymne finale, ne manquent pas d'insérer deux rondeaux chantés.[6] Cette figure poétique à reprises est considérée comme une hymne française ; le rondeau n'est pas encore partagé entre plusieurs interlocuteurs comme il le sera plus tard dans les Mystères et dans les farces où, d'ailleurs, il n'est plus chanté. C'est une singularité du *Pathelin* de n'avoir pas de rondeau ni même de

9

quatrain ni la moindre figure qui romprait avec la monotonie des octosyllabes à rimes plates.

Les chants sont très nombreux dans les grandes œuvres dramatiques du XVe siècle, mais ils sont presque exclusivement des hymnes latines. Nous distinguerons le cas de l'*Incarnation* (Rouen, 1474) (imprimé Paris, B.N. Res. Y 4349) où les douze chansons sont écrites au bas de portées musicales qui, hélas, ne sont pas pourvues de notes: le rubricateur a négligé ce travail absolument indispensable.[7] Et c'est ainsi qu'à ma connaissance, aucun manuscrit théâtral, sauf deux manuscrits de *Robin et Marion*, ne nous a transmis de la musique. Il est vrai que les mélodies des hymnes religieuses étaient bien connues.

Un cas particulier, c'est celui d'une pièce dramatique conçue à partir de chansons populaires dont plusieurs couplets sont chantés. La *Farce du Povre Jouhan* me paraît imaginée à partir de deux chansons sur Jean de Nivelle, mari berné: on aurait converti en scènes dramatiques les épisodes narrés dans des couplets à ritournelle.[8]

Les chants sont accompagnés de musique et, de plus, elles ne sont pas rares, dans les Mystères, ces pauses entre deux scènes ou marquant un arrêt de l'action, qui, dans la didascalie, sont signalées par *silete cum organis*. Par un vers de Gréban, nous savons que le *silete*, à son époque, était un chant (*et me chantez ung silete* dit Lucifer à ses diables, 3814).

5. Changements de rythme: figures métriques.

L'octosyllabe à rimes plates, on le sait, est le vers le plus banal de l'écriture littéraire dès le XIIe siècle. Toutefois, dans cette adaptation excellente de *Pirame et Tisbé*, selon les impératifs de l'expression lyrique ou tragique, le poète, rompant avec la monotonie de ces octosyllabes, recourt à des figures métriques soumises à la symétrie, certes, mais animées, par la diversité des mètres et des consonances.

De ce point de vue, nous pouvons dire que nos dramaturges et le premier, celui d'*Adam*, sont novateurs en s'étant refusé ce ronron des octosyllabes jusqu'au terme de la représentation. Le premier drame en langue française a le souci de varier le rythme en brisant la succession des vers communs par des strophes monorimes en vers plus longs empruntés au genre hagiographique. L'essentiel, pour lui, c'est de varier le débit des acteurs.

Nous n'espérions pas grand-chose de la *Résurrection du Sauveur*, plutôt fruste. Mais pourtant, au début, nous percevons quelque recherche, peu judicieuse à vrai dire: le souci de tailler des réparties de longeur égale[9] avec parfois des répétitions de rimes,[10] puis des séries de vers monorimes,[11] jusqu'à douze vers consonants.

Jean Bodel fut bien plus heureux et l'on se souvient du commentaire si pertinent de F.W. Marshall.[12] Rutebeuf aussi se mit en frais et usa pour la première fois, du couplet ou du tercet d'octosyllabes suivi du petit vers de quatre syllabes. En outre, nous trouvons, dans son Miracle, des douzains de vers de six en même temps que les quatrains monorimes déjà découverts dans *Adam*, mais ils sont ici de douze syllabes et non de dix.

Le théâtre profane, lui aussi, songe à varier le débit: un «prologue» dit par Adam de la Halle, ouvre le *Jeu de la Feuillée* en trois quatrains d'alexandrins monorimes; puis, ailleurs, sans que le changement soit commandé par le ton des répliques, nous découvrons des sixains (vv. 33-182, 837-72). Quant à son *Jeu de Robin et Marion*, les chansons suffisent à l'auteur qui ne juge pas utile de varier les vers des répliques non chantées.

Au XIVe siècle, s'accroît le souci d'alterner les modes déclamatoires; les formes métriques sont plus nombreuses encore et Mme Grace Frank eut raison d'affirmer (ed., p. VIII) «qu'aucune pièce antérieure à la *Passion de Semur* ne présente une versificatıon aussi variée que celle de la *Passion du Palatinus*.» On peut évaluer à un cinquième de l'ensemble (407 sur 1996) le nombre de vers qui ne sont pas des octosyllabes à rimes plates.

Au cours du même siècle, les modestes Miracles parisiens de Notre-Dame inaugurent une variation métrique qui, plus tard, se révélera, je l'ai dit déjà, comme plus adaptée au genre dramatique; c'est le rondeau, mais il est chanté par un chœur ou par un seul personnage. A remarquer que la seconde moitié du rondeau est le plus souvent répétée, cinquante vers plus loin. Ce procédé ingénieux donne plus de solennité à la descente du Ciel et à la remontée de la Vierge et des anges.

Au XVᵉ siècle, tous nos dramaturges connus et inconnus pratiquent «l'art de rhétorique» et Gréban, en particulier, manifestera ses talents d'acrobate du verbe, multipliant les figures et variant les mètres, de deux à dix syllabes.

6. Scènes de présentation.

Nous allons considérer à présent autre chose que le silence religieux, que les chants et les mélodies, que les rythmes et les rimes plus rapprochées qui donnaient au drame une vitalité sonore. Les scènes se suivent et chacune d'elles est localisée dans un secteur extrêmement réduit d'une scène extrêmement large, un secteur qui est différent chaque fois et que les spectateurs repèrent grâce, non pas à l'éclairage, mais aux gestes des acteurs qui s'animent pendant quelques instants. Ces conditions extérieures ont obligé nos auteurs à concevoir quelques scènes pendant lesquelles ils vont familiariser leur public avec les personnages qui, un peu plus tard, prendront part à l'action.

Ouvrons le plus ancien manuscrit de Gréban (Paris, B.N. fr. 815). La première Journée est consacrée à l'enfance du Christ. L'action paraît linéaire: annonciation, visitation, départ pour Bethléem, nativité, adoration des bergers, puis des Mages, présentation au Temple, puis voyage à Jérusalem. J'admets que des scènes préparatoires s'imposaient: l'annonce des anges aux bergers, le passage des Mages à Jérusalem chez Hérode. En outre, il fallait interrompre la biographie de Jésus pour nous montrer le massacre des Innocents. Mais ce ne sont pas ces scènes que j'envisagerai: elles sont imposées par le sujet et non par sa transposition dramatique. Je remarquerais qu'il suffisait de nous montrer des bergers interrompus dans leurs occupations ou leur sommeil par des voix célestes annonçant le Messie. Mais c'est trop peu pour notre dramaturge et trop brusque aussi. Il veut nous faire connaître ces bergers avant qu'ils n'agissent en faveur de l'action principale, avant qu'ils ne viennent adorer l'Enfant. Et nous avons cette pastorale très joyeuse de 216 vers (4620-4835), puis, cent lignes plus loin, 12 vers où, la nuit, les bergers s'encouragent à résister au sommeil (4944-55) et l'annonce des anges—la scène qui eût pu suffire—apparaît seulement deux cents vers plus loin (4147-5212). Suivra l'adoration de ces bergers (5453-5619). On pourrait s'en tenir là. Mais que faire de ces pâtres? Il n'y a pas de coulisses ou l'on pourrait les ravir à la vue; il faut une dernière scène—la cinquième—pour les ramener à leur *mansion* de départ (5632-5699). Si cet épisode des bergers de Bethléem contient cinq tranches isolées, c'est, à mon avis, parce qu'il a fallu tenir compte des nécessités de la scène. Tous les acteurs sont sur le plateau dès le début du drame ou de la Journée du Mystère. Ils ne peuvent pas quitter leur «lieu» (l'endroit où le régisseur les a placés) sans nous dire qui ils sont et cela par un dialogue (ou un monologue si l'acteur est seul). Il faut qu'on les fasse parler avant qu'ils ne se dirigent lentement vers le secteur de l'estrade où ils rencontreront d'autres personnages pour participer à l'action centrale. Enfin, il faut une autre scène parlée pour leur donner le loisir de regagner le lieu qui leur est assigné.

On aperçoit donc pourquoi et comment ce théâtre médiéval, qui n'a pas les coulisses de nos scènes modernes, est forcé de faire précéder et de faire suivre de scènes particulières l'épisode où des personnages interviennent dans l'action amorcée par d'autres. Pour les bergers de Bethléem, deux scènes suffiraient à un dramaturge moderne, moyennant un changement de décors; pour un dramaturge médiéval, quatre scènes étaient obligatoires et Gréban nous en a donné cinq. On objectera que le prédecesseur de Gréban, Eustache Marcadé s'était contenté de deux tranches pour l'adoration des bergers (1624-1702 2130-2363). Deux tranches oui, mais la deuxième compte quatre scènes, en somme, car, sans interruption, nous voyons les bergers surpris par les anges, s'avancer vers Bethléem, adorer l'Enfant, puis s'en retourner en dialoguant.

Il y a aussi des circonstances qu'il faut évoquer et, pour qu'on s'en souvienne, il ne suffit pas d'une allusion: les auteurs ont voulu des scènes à part. Considérons le recensement impérial qui motiva le départ de Joseph et de Marie pour Bethléem. C'est bien une circonstance déterminante et rien que cela: l'Évangile de saint Luc le mentionne, mais ne le décrit pas. Nos dramaturges, et Eustache Marcadé, en particulier, ont jugé qu'il fallait présenter le recensement comme un sujet à développer. Marcadé introduit l'empereur dictant un édit à son héraut (1516-1623), puis celui-ci arrivant à Jérusalem et transmettant ses lettres à «l'évêque» Cirin qui les fait lire au peuple (elles sont en prose: 1703-1818), pui rentrant à Rome sans mot dire. On s'attendrait dès lors à voir Joseph se présenter aux recenseurs puisque c'est pour cela qu'il s'est rendu à Bethléem. Mais non, l'auteur n'en parle pas, parce que l'Évangile n'a pas donné cette scène. Par contre, si Marcadé a imaginé une scène à Rome et une autre à Jérusalem chez Cirin, c'est pour que les spectateurs sachent ce qu'est ce recensement, pourquoi Joseph et Marie ont fait le voyage et pourquoi ils n'ont pas trouvé à se loger à Bethléem.

Arnould Gréban qui, certes, a connu la *Passion d'Arras*, a signalé ce recensement, mais d'une manière plus simple. Il a renoncé à nous montrer l'empereur à Rome, mais il a conservé une scène à Jérusalem ou Cirinus, prévôt de Judée., charge son messager Légeret d'aller diffuser l'édit impérial (4263-4356). Un peu plus loin, une courte scène va permettre à Légeret de réintégrer le palais de Cirinus (4425-4444). Mais, si Gréban réduit à 114 vers ce qui en comptait 224 chez Marcadé, il recourt au moyen qui eût suffi à l'écrivain moderne: l'allusion. L'un des bergers amuse ses compagnons en leur disant les opérations étranges auxquelles on vient de le soumettre à Bethléem: on comprend qu'on l'a forcé à déclarer son nom à l'agent recenseur (4772-4821). A vrai dire, cette allusion eût mieux convenu lorsque Joseph cherchait un logis à Bethléem.

7. Scènes de remplissage.

Le lecteur d'un Mystère s'étonne de voir certaines scènes interrompues par de brefs dialogues qui sont entendus devant une autre *mansion*. On peut croire qu'on a voulu déplacer souvent le pôle d'attention, car, pendant une scène, les yeux des spectateurs étaient retenus par tel secteur de l'estrade qui n'était peut-être pas en face, mais si éloigné qu'il fallait se tourner de côté pour l'observer. Je songe aux *mansions* extrêmes comme le Paradis ou l'Enfer. Mais précisément les scènes célestes ou diaboliques sont parmi les plus longues: ce qui prouverait que les auteurs ne se souciaient guère de la gêne des spectateurs des premiers rangs. Ce qui est assuré, c'est que la succession relativement rapide des scènes a permis à l'auteur de déplacer fréquemment le centre d'intérêt, j'entends l'endroit de la longue estrade où il se passe quelque chose.

L'absence de coulisses provoque ce fait capital; rien ne nous est caché de ce que devient un acteur depuis le moment où il quitte son lieu jusqu'au moment où il y retourne. Et donc, quand un acteur passe d'une *mansion* à l'autre, pendant le temps conventionnel qui serait celui d'un trajet en ville ou d'un voyage, ou bien l'acteur doit monologuer ou converser avec un compagnon, ou bien une autre scène, ailleurs, occupe le temps qu'on accorde à ce déplacement.

Cette scène peut être de remplissage. Parfois, si l'auteur est habile, cette scène avancera une action bientôt convergente, en pratiquant le procédé de l'entrelacement, en usage dans le roman.

Scène de remplissage aussi que cette répétition d'un message. Prenons, chez Gréban, l'exemple de la comparution de Joseph d'Arimathie devant les Juifs. Ceux-ci, jugeant que Joseph leur a fait affront en ensevelissant Jésus, décident de le citer devant leur tribunal et, pour ce faire, appellent cinq soldats et les chargent de s'emparer de l'inculpé (27587-27902). Tandis que ces soldats s'acheminent là où se trouve Joseph, Gréban nous impose une courte scène de 68 vers (27903-70) nous montrant les trois Maries partant acheter des parfums: elle est bien inutile pour l'action, cette scène-là, mais celle est requise par le régisseur:

1º il faut que, dès le moment où les Maries entament un mouvement, elles commencent à parler;

2º il faut qu'on parle quelque part pendant le temps conventionnel qu'on réserve aux soldats pour trouver Joseph.

Ils s'adressent à lui et lui disent des choses désagréables tout en le poussant vers le tribunal (27971-28006): 36 vers inutiles si nous avions à représenter cet épisode avec les moyens de notre époque. En effet, on aurait vu un Caïphe confier une mission à des soldats qui auraient disparu dans les coulisses et qui en seraient revenus plus tard avec Joseph. Entretemps, les Juifs sur scène auraient eu à avancer l'action, par exemple, en interrogeant les soldats du

15

Sépulchre qui ont vu que le tombeau du Christ avait été vidé. Or, Gréban ne peut parler de cette affaire que bien plus tard. Ainsi donc, l'action avance très lentement sur le plateau où se déroulent les drames médiévaux et cela est du principalement à la mise en scène simultanée qui ne permet pas la soustraction des inutilités comme le font nos coulisses.

8. Scènes de détente.

Autrefois, Gaston Paris, opposant les Miracles dramatiques aux Mystères, considérait que ceux-ci, «gênés par la sainteté même de l'action qu'ils représentaient ne pouvaient prendre aucune liberté et étaient emprisonnés dans des données surnaturelles exclusives de tout intérêt vraiment humain.»[13] Ces lignes ont été écrites en 1880-1881, cinq ans après que Gastron Paris eut signé l'édition du *Mystère de la Passion* d'Arnoul Gréban, œuvre qu'il n'a jamais aimée. Il l'a dit en 1878: «ouvrage considérable, travaillé, mais où il est impossible de reconnaître du génie ou même un talent remarquable.»[14] Assurément, les Mystères,—et a fortiori les Mystères de la Passion,—ont à traiter un sujet sacré dont on ne peut s'écarter sans péril. Lorsqu'en 1456, à Angers, un auteur fait copier son Mystère de la *Résurrection*, c'est après avoir soustrait ce que des acteurs avaient ajouté, de leur propre initiative, au rôle qu'on leur avait assigné et avaient provoqué de ce fait les foudres des théologiens de l'Université.

Mais, prenons-y garde, le respect scrupuleux des textes sacrés peut s'accommoder d'un accueil généreux offert aux légendes pieuses. Dans ce Mystère de la *Résurrection*, les théologiens sévères d'Angers, qui ont contrôlé une seconde édition du texte (l'auteur le dit explicitement), n'ont pas trouvé condamnable ce qu'on a ajouté aux Évangiles: le procès de Joseph d'Arimathie, les contestations des Juifs et de Pilate avec les soldats du Sépulcre, et surtout le rôle étendu attribué à Carinus et à Léoncius, fils du vieillard Siméon, ressuscités le jour de la mort du Christ. Parmi ces trois additions, la seconde que Gréban même s'est permise aussi, a un caractère purement humain: les gardiens du Sépulcre doivent sortir d'un mauvais pas puisqu'ils auraient mal surveillé le tombeau.

Aussi, ils menacent les Juifs de proclamer que le Christ est ressuscité et, sachant par ailleurs que Joseph a été délivré et reste introuvable, ils proposent au Conseil des Juifs de livrer Jésus si on parvient à leur montrer Joseph. C'est un défi et les Juifs doivent bien accepter de payer grassement le mensonge qu'ils exigent de ces Romains finauds. Cette scène nous prouve que, sans porter atteinte à la dignité du drame sacré, on pouvait descendre du sublime au sérieux. Et volontairement, les auteurs ont voulu farcir leurs Mystères de familier et même de comique. Leur intention a été exprimée sans ambages:

1º dans les *Miracles de Sainte-Geneviève* de la fin du XIVe siècle: «Cy après sont autres miracles de madame sainte Genevieve. Sachiez que chaccun emporte plusieurs personnages (*rôles*) de plusieurs malades pour cause de brieté, et a parmy farsses entees, afin que le jeu soit mains fades et plus plaisans»;[15]

2º dans le Mystère de la *Résurrection* d'Angers (1456):

> Aussi y sont, par intervales,
> d'aucuns esbatemens et galles
> d'un aveugle et de son varlet
> que gueres ne servent au fait
> si ce n'est pour vous resjouïr
> et vos esperis rafreschir. (MS Chantilly, 86 rº et vº);

3º dans le Mystère de l'*Incarnation* de Rouen (14747). On y trouve un récit bouffon et l'auteur, en marge, nous prie de l'en excuser:

«Ista narratio ponatur hic ad sublevandum animos audientium.»[16] Il est donc certain que les auteurs ont eu pitié de leur public à qui ils imposaient des séances de 5000 vers le matin, puis de 5000 autres dans l'après-midi avec une interruption d'une demi-heure à peine pour dîner! Les dramaturges se rendaient compte que leur œuvre requérait un grand effort d'attention, de compréhension, d'abstraction, et que le public, dans sa majorité, n'était pas assis. C'est pourquoi, ils ont voulu recréer leur auditoire par intermittence. Comment l'ont-ils fait?

Les auteurs les plus graves comme Gréban, se sont contentés

1º de changer de registre, d'insérer du lyrisme profane dans un épisode obligatoire comme la «bergerie», où on exalterait le bonheur de la vie aux champs. Jean Michel, de son côté, nous séduit par la mondanité de Madeleine pécheresse.

2º On concède beaucoup aux traditions déjà vieilles qui exigent que tous les messagers soient ivrognes, que les épiciers soient charlatans, que les soldats soient fanfarons, que les démoniaques profèrent des obscénités. Dès qu'on les voit surgir, le public s'apprête à rire et l'auteur n'oserait pas le décevoir.

3º D'autres auteurs, et ce sont peut-être les moins habiles, ont eu recours à la farce qui, semble-t-il, signifiait aussi «moquerie.» On en a inséré dans des drames pieux, même très courts comme le *Jeu de saint Fiacre* (1256 vers): «Cy est interposé une farsse», à savoir une bagarre entre maris et femmes (280 vers). A Angers, en 1456, un anonyme fait mieux ancore: il insère, dans la 2e et la 3e Journée de sa *Résurrection,* une farce de 1400 vers environ, offerte en cinq tranches, n'ayant presque aucune adhérence au drame et consacrée aux tours plaisants et ingénieux qu'un valet joue à son patron aveugle et méfiant. Quatorze cents vers de pur divertissement sur un total de vingt mille!

TELLES sont les particularités du texte dramatique en général dont on trouve la raison d'être dans l'œuvre elle-même, à savoir le déroulement d'activités simulées par des hommes se disant autres et parlant comme s'ils n'étaient pas eux, j'ai dit la représentation théâtrale même, différente de la nôtre, plus longue que nos spectacles. Ces particularités qu'on n'aperçoit pas de prime abord sont recueillies dans le théâtre religieux dont le répertoire compte des œuvres de larges dimensions; le théâtre profane est bien plus modeste et on n'y perçoit guère ces nécessités de satisfaire diversément les spectateurs.

Dans ces deux théâtres, il existe certaines habitudes formelles qu'on interprète comme des adjuvants de l'exécution. Tout d'abord, remarquons l'enchaînement des répliques par la rime dite *mnémonique.* C'est le nom qu'ont donné les critiques à une rime chevauchante unissant le dernier vers d'une réplique au premier vers de la réplique suivante. On suppose qu'un acteur, en entendant son interlocuteur s'arrêter sur un vers à rime *c*, se rappellera le début de sa répartie commençant précisément par un vers à rime *c*. Le procédé a été excellemment étudié par W. Noomen, surtout dans le jeu de *Saint Nicolas* qui est le premier à le présenter.[17] Remarquons toutefois que ce concept de rime mnémonique est le fait des observateurs modernes; nous n'en sommes pas informés par les arts poétiques de l'époque. On pourrait croire que ce que l'on considère comme un appel à la répartie n'est qu'un procédé d'écriture, un enchaînement de deux textes en octosyllabes à rimes plates, d'autant plus que cette rime mnémonique n'existait pas, avant le XVe siècle, lorsqu'il y avait un changement de versification. L'examen du jeu de *Saint Nicolas* ne nous convainc pas que l'enchaînement des répliques par la rime ait vraiment une virtualité mnémonique, sollicite vraiment la mémoire de l'acteur qui doit avancer sa réplique. Aujourd'hui, un souffleur chuchote les *premiers* mots d'une réplique...Et puis, dans Jean Michel, la Quarte Journée est unie à la Tierce par la même rime: cette liaison ne sert pas aux acteurs, assurément pas.

Par contre, au XIVe siècle, apparaît un procédé significatif qui aura, hélas, disparu au XVe. Dans 39 *Miracles de Notre-Dame*, plusieurs auteurs terminent chaque réplique en vers octosyllabiques, par une clausule de quatre syllabes présentant une rime qui est reprise par la réplique suivante Dans ces pièces-là, l'acteur, entendant son interlocuteur *briser* son rythme, sait qu'est bien arrivé son tour de prendre la parole. On peut se demander d'ailleurs si ce petit vers n'est pas hérité du couplet ou du tercet d'octosyllabes suivi d'un vers de quatre sur une autre rime que l'on rencontre dans le *Miracle de Théophile* de Rutebeuf; mais chez lui, c'est une figure métrique, tandis que, dans des chansons de geste du Cycle de Guillaume, il se présente en fin de laisse comme une clausule du chant.

RÉSUMONS-NOUS.

LES TEXTES conservés, qu'ils soient destinés à la lecture ou à une représentation théâtrale, ne produisent que ce qui a été dit sur la scène et, sommairement, relatent ce qu'on y a fait. Le texte est loin d'être toute l'œuvre dramatique.

Nous imaginant vivre ces longues heures de spectacle, nous pouvons découvrir, dans nos manuscrits ou dans nos imprimés, de nombreux caractères qui ne se justifient, semble-t-il, que par des nécessités scéniques et des concessions à un public qu'on ne ménageait guère. Nous percevons ces nécessités de créer le silence et ensuite une atmosphère religieuse jusque par delà la représentation. Pour plaire, il faut varier : d'où ces changements de tons et de figures métriques, ces chants et ces mélodies.

D'autre part, la succession et le choix des scènes sont commandés évidemment par le sujet, mais aussi par des nécessités scéniques. Tous les acteurs qui ont à jouer au cours de la séance sont vus de tous dès le début. Avant de les amener jusqu'à l'endroit de la scène où ils auront à intervenir, l'auteur doit les faire parler là où ils sont. Ensuite, il doit éviter les temps morts en remplissant la durée conventionnelle d'un trajet. Enfin, il faut distraire le public soit en lui servant des personnages comiques traditionnels, soit en lui offrant des scènes très profanes, soit encore en truffant le drame sacré d'une farce pleine de gros sel.

Ces servitudes contribuent à allonger la pièce, la rendent moins dense et même prolixe, empêchent toute unité de ton, même s'il s'agit d'une tragédie sainte comme la Passion. Mais, à moins d'être trop sévère, on peut goûter encore les variations fréquentes et inattendues de ces Mystères qui nous paraissent un cosmos hétéroclite semblable à l'humanité.

NOTES

1. J'ai cru pouvoir le prouver dans mon article sur «Le théâtre médiéval et sa transmission par le livre», *Research Studies*, 32 (1964). 63–75.

2. Édité par Pierre Le Verdier , 3 vols. (Rouen, 1884-1886 [*Société des Bibliophiles Normands*]). Voir aussi *Le Livre de Conduite du régisseur...* pour le *Mystère de la Passion* joué à Mons en 1501, publié par G. Cohen (Strasbourg, 1925).

3. *Histoire de la mise en scène dans le théâtre religieux du moyen âge* (Paris, 1926).

4. Voir mon édition du *Mystère de la Passion* de Jean Michel (Gembloux, 1959), p. xli.

5. Dans la *Romania* 89 (1968). 145–93.

6. On remarque, chaque fois, cette exhortation: *chantons* (ce *rondel*...). Pourtant, on ne trouve que *disons* (n°V 278), mais si, au vers 500 du même Miracle, on annonce aussi le rondeau par *disons*, la reprise est lancée par *chantant* 582 et *chant* 587,

7. Voir l'édition P. Le Verdier, 3, pp. xvi–xvii.

8. Voir mon compte rendu dans *Les Lettres Romanes* 15 (1961). 291–94.

9. Quatre, puis six, puis huit vers (MS Paris 29–72).

10. Vers 29–32, 33–36.

11. Vers 57–64, 65–68, 113–16, 117–20, 133–36, 197–200, 201–4, 205–8, 209–12, 227–34, 235–38, 255–66, 297–300, 301–4, 307–10.

12. "The Rhyme Schemes of the *Jeu de Saint Nicolas* as an Indication of Staging," *Australian Journal of French Studies* 1 (1964). 225–6. "The Staging of the *Jeu de Saint Nicolas;* an Analysis of Movement," Ibid., 2 (1965).

13. *La littérature française du moyen âge*, 7e ed. (Paris), pp. 268–69.

14. P. XVI de l'Introduction.

15. Édition d'A. Jubinal, *Mystères inédits du quinzième siècle*, 1 (Paris, 1837), p. 281.

16. Édition P. Le Verdier, 2, 254.

17. Dans *Neophilologus* 40 (1956).

TRADITION AND ORIGINALITY
IN THE MEDIEVAL DRAMA
IN GERMANY

Wolfgang Michael

ORIGINALITY in the medieval German drama! Perhaps you will say there is no such thing. Does not the development of this form unfold before us like the slow constant growth of a plant? From the early beginnings, from the *Quem quaeritis* trope, still undramatic, to the first drama of the *Visitatio*, to the simple Latin Easter play, to the Easter play in the vernacular, to the encompassing Passion play, and finally to the cyclic panoramic presentation of the late Middle Ages and the Renaissance, including everything from creation to doomsday? Where in all this stream of theatrical activity is there the originality of the individual, of the real dramatist?

But perhaps a closer look will reveal that this development is not always quite so simple, quite so smooth as it may appear at first. Let us recapitulate the first stages. We all know the embryo from which the drama grew is that famous Easter trope, the *Quem quaeritis*, sung at the introit of the Mass, perhaps as Young suggested, the work of Tutilo of St. Gall, the great student of Notker.[1] We also know from reading Young that in this position, in the Mass, this highly dramatic piece never could, or at least never did, develop into drama. Rather, it had to be separated from this service and be attached to Matins before drama originated. But why was this trope separated from the Mass? Why was it attached to Matins? Why did it develop later into drama in that new position? Young has no explanation. In an article almost completely overlooked, Jude Woerdeman furnished answers to these questions.[2] From Carolingian times there were constant efforts to unify the liturgy, to adopt the Roman usage in all parts of Christendom. These efforts had to overcome the strong resistance of monastic forces who preferred their own dear time-honored forms. At Matins on Easter day, according to the Benedictine rule, a lesson from the Gospel was read after the *Te Deum*. The lesson taken from the Gospel of St. Mark describes the visit of the Marys to the sepulchre and only this event. This reading of the Gospel lesson was not part of the Roman usage; rather it was frowned upon. In a synod in Winchester in the latter half of the tenth century Roman usage won, but not without a significant compromise. For the eliminated Gospel reading, *Quem quaeritis* was substituted, but not in the plain undramatic form of the trope, rather in the form of the *Visitatio*.

So far we were following Woerdeman's presentation. But if Woerdeman's argumentation is correct, and it seems quite convincing, then we can, then we must draw other far-reaching conclusions. Not only would we know why the transfer from Mass to Matins was made; we would also know that this transfer was not some gradual process but a unique act; that before, there was no drama; that it is no accident that the *Regularis Concordia,* the out-growth of the Winchester synod, contains the first and the only early documentation for the drama in the Middle Ages; in short, that the authors of the *Regularis Concordia* were the creators of medieval drama. After all, the time span between trope and *Visitatio*—perhaps only a few decades—seems too short for a gradual process.[3] After all, the *Regularis Concordia* was not just one of the innumerable ordinaries that contained the locally limited liturgical traditions. It was the rule book for the entire Benedictine order in England, the order that mainly, and at first almost exclusively, performed the religious drama. Representatives from the Continent participated in the synod. It is easy to understand how through them and through the international exchange among monasteries this new usage spread to other countries, developed further and then acquired local peculiarities.

If our argumentation is correct, the medieval drama began through an original act well prepared through the development of the trope, but an original act after all.

We know that from then on the presentations of the *Visitatio* became a general western tradition. It has been shown recently that from area to area differences in detail existed.[4] But they were minor; they did not break the overwhelming unity of the form. Embellishments were introduced. Wipo's striking «Victimae Paschali» was absorbed into the drama. Traditions at other feast days developed, so to speak, in the shadow of the *Visitatio*. In France the Fleury play collection testifies for lively and not entirely unoriginal activities. In France Abelard's versatile disciple, Hilarius, composed or at least arranged a number of interesting playlets. In France, the *Jeu d'Adam*, quite outside of tradition, is proof of an amazingly early rise of the drama in the vernacular. The Monte Cassino fragments show that Italy preceded all other countries in the transition to the passion play. Are there no signs of such activities in Germany?

Perhaps the most unusual single Latin religious drama is the so-called Tegernsee *Antichrist*.[5] As far as we know, there was no tradition that stimulated or even preceded this drama. Nor did it form the root of any Antichrist family tree. The far later treatments of this theme show no similarity beyond the traits of the common topic, nothing of the ingenious spirit of the Tegernesee creation.

The dating of the Tegernsee *Antichrist* has been the subject of considerable controversy. There is a hundred-year discrepancy in the dating of this document. Historical allusions were interpreted as referring to this or that event. These allusions seem too vague to be a safe guide in the dating. There is only one clue that offers greater certainty. Gerhoh of Reichersberg, a religious activist, in his tract *"De investigatione Antichristi"* of 1161, attacked plays in the church as sinful and blasphemous.[6] He mentioned specifically, performances of Christmas plays and an Antichrist. Did he refer to the Tegernsee Play? We know of no other Antichrist drama of the time. Some of the self-righteous demands of the *hypocritae*, the venomous advisers of Antichrist, sound like quotations from Gerhoh's earlier works. Reichersberg, where Gerhoh lived when he wrote his treatise, is quite close to Tegernsee. In short, it seems very likely that Gerhoh referred to our drama. But even if this is not the case, the work, we can say, is the first political drama of the Middle Ages. It has always been asserted that there were strong nationalistic undertones in the *Antichrist*. That is true to a certain extent: the emperor and the Germans are shown in a highly favorable light, but the *Antichrist* is far more an attack on religious zealots. As in the time of the Reformation, the adversary was Antichrist. The Catholics called Luther the Antichrist, the Lutherans called the Pope the Antichrist. Who is the *clericus* who used this sharp and piercing weapon for the first time against religious self-righteous bigotry? Was he a *vagans* who saw his own free human way of life endangered? Is the Tegernsee *Antichrist* the first document in Germany of the invasion by the *vagantes* into the firm tradition of the liturgical drama? No matter who the author was his work is a monument to his genius. Although he used an earlier narrative as his source material he treated it with an ease of superior ability. For the first time in medieval drama we find a well-planned structure; we find real characters—from the venomous *hypocritae*, to the opportunistic French king, to the German emperor, brave and faithful, but slightly stupid. We find a mastery of language and metric forms quite unheard of in the previous Latin drama in Germany.

We mentioned before that the Tegernsee Ludus did not start a tradition of Antichrist dramas; yet this play was not completely without effect on the following medieval Latin drama. In one of the plays of the Benediktbeuren collection, there are lengthy passages lifted verbatim or nearly verbatim from the Tegernsee Ludus. The Benediktbeuren piece is a fragment called by Young "Ludus de Rege Egypti."[7] It deals with the flight to Egypt and the falling of the idols. It may or may not be part of the Benediktebeuren Christmas play. Spring songs, a call "ad fontem philosophiae" and then, taken from Tegernsee, an amazingly objective description of the pagan, the polytheistic view. This fragment is perhaps the clearest expression of the spirit that pervades all the dramas of the Benediktbeuren collection, the spirit of enjoyment of life and yet also of piety, of admiration for learning and also of crudeness and frivolity, a sense for the finesse of Latin style and of enjoyment of the vulgarity of the vernacular. We sense the spirit of the *clerici vagantes*, of the goliards, as they are generally called in English.

The Benediktbeuren collection is the most outstanding vagantic collection on German soil. Poetry and drama, Latin and bits of German and even French often in a macaronic mixture, love poetry frequently frivolous and again deeply religious poetry—that is the colorful array of this work gathered perhaps for an art loving, dignified clergyman. How did the spirit of this collection, the spirit of vagantic literature, influence, transform the tradition of the liturgical drama?

Ever since the days of the *Regularis Concordia*, the *Visitatio* expanded, included new scenes, used new details. Feast days other than Easter, such as Christmas, Epiphany, the Day of the Innocent Children were embellished with similar playlets. But with few exceptions these documents show a steady tradition, mostly bound to specific areas. From area to area, from bishopric to bishopric we recognize specific local peculiarities. The Benediktbeuren documents are quite different. I am not referring to the frequent German interpolations—German text had intruded before. Nor does the greater finesse in metric, in stylistic devices, or even a stronger sense of characterization indicate a complete break with tradition, although all these elements together do weigh heavily. But in addition to these features, the Benediktbeuren plays attain a complexity of representation by bringing together traditional topics into a larger cycle, like the Easter play, like the Christmas play. And in the passion plays an entirely new theme, never used before nor after north of the Alps in the liturgical drama was included. In the larger passion play, just as in the previously mentioned[5] *Ludus de Rege Egypti*, vagantic joy of life is portrayed eloquently in the somewhat extraneous scenes of Maria Magdalene. Before, scenes like the race of the apostles to the sepulchre, the raging of Herod in the Christmas play had afforded a certain comic relief. But Maria Magdalene's love song, her pride in her beauty, show an enjoyment of life unknown to the earlier religious drama. We can observe here a striking phenomenon: the worldly part of the drama is echoed in a number of later Easter plays in the vernacular, while other scenes in these same plays exhibit no similarity whatsoever. In an earlier treatise I deduced from this fact that the *vagantes* had, so to speak, their own repertory of worldly scenes; that on their wanderings, wherever they were permitted to do so, they would insert these scenes into the regular stock of the religious performances.[8] This would explain why in the Benediktbeuren passion the Maria Magdalene scenes in sheer bulk completely overshadow the rest of the play. It would explain why in the later so-called Erlau collection of plays there is a separate Maria Magdalene play in the vernacular.[9] This same spirit of worldly joy is most noticeable in the so-called mercator scene, the scene where the Marys buy their ointments. This simple scene, the mere acquisition of ointments, quickly took on surprising dimensions and lost almost all of its original religious character. The merchant was soon transformed into the timeless figure of the quack doctor. His assistant was not only well versed in all the shoddy tricks of salesmanship, but also told innumerable vulgar jokes. He finally ran away with his employer's amorous but quarrelsome wife. These scenes, completely alien to the dignified, the deeply religious and predominantly serious tenor of the liturgical drama, have long been recognized as the work of the *clerici vagantes*. Tradition has all but disappeared. A freshness and ingenuity pervades this coarse humor which I would like to call original. In any case the *clerici* helped to overcome some limitations of the liturgical drama. They may have been responsible for the introduction of the vernacular. They helped to transform the medieval drama; for a while this drama showed a new form.

We have seen how the medieval drama developed from an original act of creation. Liturgical tradition absorbed it and developed it until the vagantic spirit gave it new forms, new possibilities. Still, the clergy remained predominant in the performances. In the late thirteenth, in the fourteenth and fifteenth centuries, a gradual transformation took place. The twelfth and thirteenth centuries had been the great epoch of courtly and knightly epic and lyric poetry. German drama shows no trace of courtly or knightly influence. The castles were perhaps not the right stages for religious performances, although we do know that in the thirteenth century a passion play was performed on the Wartburg before Count Louis of Thuringia, and in 1321 a play of the wise and foolish virgins was performed in Eisenach before Count Frederick. But both plays were enacted by clerics. Now at the end of the thirteenth century, a new base for dramatic presentations appeared. Around castles and market places cities had formed. Craftsmen developed special skills that previously in their cruder form had been common possession. Their manufactures gave impetus to increased trading. Knighthood lost its military significance. The cities gained in political, in economic, in cultural stature. Some were only important centers inside a larger political structure. Others developed their own political structure; as Freie Reichsstädte they became independent, subject only to the emperor. In these centers new religious dramas originated. In northern Tirol, salt mining gained more and more importance; in the cities in the south of Tirol, horticulture and the production of wine created wealth. The whole area, north and south of the Brenner pass, became a single unit in performances of religious dramas.[10]

Lucerne, canton and city, was one of the original areas that gained independence from Austria. Important as access city to the Gotthard pass, it became one of the centers of Swiss economic and cultural activity. A passion play developed here that was later adapted by the old Black Forest town, Villingen, then still under Austrian domination.[11]

Frankfurt, a powerful independent city where the emperors were crowned, crossing point of the north-south trade route along the Rhine and the east-west trade route along the Main River and a leading commercial community, became the focus of religious performances.[12] We can trace the origins of the plays in Frankfurt back to the thirteenth century. They were performed until the advent of the Reformation. Plays related to the Frankfurt passion were performed in the whole west middle German area in Mainz, in Friedberg, in Fritzlar, in Marburg , and as far northeast as the town of Alsfeld, approximately 90 km. from Frankfurt.[13]

The plays in these three centers again show the force of tradition, but in a different way. While the liturgical drama developed in monastery churches, this new drama began in cathedrals and frequently moved into the market places because the sheer bulk of action demanded a larger area. While the language of the liturgical drama, even with all the vagantic extravagances, remained chiefly Latin, this new drama was written almost entirely in the vernacular. While the liturgical drama was entirely or mostly performed by the clergy, the new drama was more and more taken over by the city administration; the craftsmen, the guilds performed it. The text is transferred largely by oral tradition; it has become folk drama in the true sense of the word. To be sure, while in the liturgical drama (at least in Germany) the authors remained unknown, in the folk drama in the fifteenth and sixteenth century the names of a few outstanding figures have been preserved to us. In Tirol, Benedikt Debs, the schoolmaster, and his friend Vigil Raber, the painter, were involved in many performances: in Lucerne, Hans Salat, Zacharias Bletz, and later Renward Cysat directed, supervised, stimulated the presentations; the Corpus Christi plays in Freiburg i. B. were for years in the able hands of Hans Baldung, a relative of the famous painter. It is obvious that all these men left their mark on text and presentation. Yet they were not authors; they were subservient in the real meaning of this word to a greater world that came to them and that went on after them—the world of tradition. Aside from their activity as directors or participants in the passion plays, they may have been authors, dramatists in their own right, as for instance Bletz and Salat actually were. And their own dramas show a certain amount of ability and originality. Yet, in their activity in the passion play, the spirit of the work seemed stronger than they were (they were, as we said, subservient). Not that these plays were great artistic masterpieces: for the modern reader most of their scenes are trite, repetitious, sentimental; they are clumsy in language and metric form, illogical in structure, colorless in characterization. Surely those naughty vagantic extravagances appear far superior in quality. However, in the passion plays, the reverence before time-honored customs, the spirit of tradition was stronger than any individual impulse. Let me use the example of the Freiburg Corpus Christi play to show that even if the text may have undergone variations and changes, the force of tradition was maintained.

The earliest documents of the Freiburg Corpus Christi play are two "Ordnungen," lists which simply indicate the order in which the various scenes were performed; they do not contain any spoken dialogue. These "Ordnungen" were written down possibly in 1516; they are dated for this year and we have evidence that about this time the text was imported from Bozen in Tirol, where it had flourished.[14] During the first half of the century there are references to performances in the council books; also a few textual fragments are preserved, the texts of separate scenes as they were performed by the individual guilds or other city organizations. The oldest of these fragments comprises the Christmas scenes and is probably as old as the "Ordnungen." Entries in the city ledgers and in the council minutes make it evident that during the entire first half of the century, the text as a whole had not been written down; the individual scene texts were the only ones in existence. Not until 1576 did a certain Hatzenberger "put all the speeches of the play together into a book," as the city council minutes put it. The oldest entire text extant is dated 1599, but the innumerable changes in the text—cuts and far more often additions, sometimes very lengthy additions, alterations, transpositions—indicate that this text had served for many performances; that it had been written down much earlier; that it is most likely the Hatzenberger text of 1576. If we study the changes of this and if we compare the text with the earlier scene texts, we can recognize how tradition transforms the drama. Often the changes are made to give greater detail; sometimes we suspect that a specific actor demanded more lines; sometimes technical difficulties may have required the changes; sometimes the director may have wanted to show a new technical trick. The transpositions do not always result in what we would now call a more logical arrangement; sometimes we simply cannot explain the reason for the change. What we see here is purely folk drama, although it is different from folksong in that it is at least partially based on written rather than oral tradition. The laws of change are very similar, but perhaps we should not speak of laws, rather of lawlessness.

In places like Tirol, Lucerne, Frankfrut, Freiburg and others, long tradition predominated. But were there no other plays with a more unique history, plays by an individual author, even if his name has not been preserved, plays which did not grow out of tradition or which did not create one?

The most outstanding example for such a German play and perhaps the finest drama of its period, if we can apply aesthetic judgments, is the Easter play of Muri.[15] It is preserved only in fragmentary form. From the language we must assume that it was written in the thirteenth century in northeast Switzerland, perhaps in the very Muri where it was found. It is the only vernacular religious drama from this early period extant in Germany. But it is not unique solely because of this fact. Text and structure are quite different in character from all the other earlier or later plays. It is the only early Easter play that shows no textual similarity with other dramas. Nor does it show any of the customary clichés in either structure or content. Its metric form is much closer to the courtly epic with its relatively versatile four stress line than to the *Knüttelvers*, the German doggerel of the later religious dramas. No unevenness in the text betrays the transformational power of repeated performances. In short, we suspect that this play was written for just one performance; it has all the traits of originality.

There are a few other unique plays, even if not from an early period. The so-called Redentin Easter play from the late fifteenth century, probably performed in Lübeck, contains a lengthy descent to Hell with an unusually colorful satire of medieval life.[16] However, similar scenes did occur in other Easter plays, particularly in those where we suspect the participation of the *clerici vagantes*.

In general, tradition seems to have been such a powerful force in the religious drama of the late Middle Ages that no one was able to escape it. The drama was so widespread that everyone must have been familiar with the customary scenes, the customary characters, even some of the oft repeated rhymes. Let me give an example that shows this all-pervading force of tradition.

In Lucerne an Easter play text was found, dated 1494 and with the heading "editus per Mathiam Gundelfinger." For a while this was considered the early version of the Lucerne passion. Brandstetter, who, in his loving devotion to the history of his home town, gave the first and detailed account of the play and its performances, thought the text was the Lucerne *Urspiel*.[17] Yet, since there was absolutely no textual similarity between the Gundelfinger play and the later Lucerne passion, this theory had to be discarded. Almost by accident the origin of the Gundelfinger play was determined. Gundelfinger, member of a well known southwest German family, was canon in the little town of Zurzach on the South, the Swiss bank of the Rhine. All the other actors, whose names were scribbled on the manuscript, were Zurzachians. We do not know how the text was brought to Lucerne, but it is clear our good friend Gundelfinger wrote it for the performance in Zurzach and directed it.[18] And this performance was probably never repeated. To be exact, it is not an Easter play; it depicts in its fragmentary form the descent from the cross and the interment. So it was an original play written by an author known to us and on a special topic? Yes and no. Although, as we said, there are no textual similarities with other plays; although it does not belong to any stemma, Gundelfinger's work is not, like the play from Muri, unique in its spirit. Of course, all plays follow their Biblical and apocryphal sources; but now, at the end of the Middle Ages, far beyond mere thematic dependency, it was almost impossible to write an original Easter play. Gundelfinger's work is proof of that. There are, we said, no textual similarities with other works; but the whole tenor, the stereotype characters, the meticulous attention to detail (everything must be played out), the simple *Knüttelvers* that impresses by its very lack of refinement; the simple narrative style, unspiced by any sentimentalities; these are the traits of all religious folk dramas of the time. It is not just the style of the time. The carnival plays, the Humanist dramas of exactly the same period, could develop an entirely different dramatic form, a different dramatic language. Authors like Burkard Waldis, like Niklaus Manuel, like Blathasar Spross from Zürich, author of the "Spiel von den alten und jungen Eidgenossen," worked quite differently. And at least Waldis also used Biblical material. Their dramas may have serious artistic limitations; we may consider them less impressive than some of the religious plays of the time; yet no doubt they are original; they do not follow a tradition.

We spoke of carnival plays, of Humanist dramas. The Humanist dramas, although first written and performed in the late fifteenth century, herald a new age, and so we can disregard them. But the carnival plays, the Fastnachtspiele that sprang up in the early fifteenth century, certainly express the medieval spirit, even if it is only the spirit of the late Middle Ages.[19] We need not discuss the origin of this genre, hidden from us in a cloud of uncertainty and scholarly controversy. Nor do we plan a "Wesensbestimmung" of these light, naughty and playful little pieces. But our theme —originality vs. tradition—can well be applied to these playlets.

There seems to be only one safe definition of Fastnachtspiele. They are little dramatic or semidramatic pieces that were performed at Fastnacht, at the time of prelenten, prefasting boisterousness and extravaganza. The large majority of these pieces show not much more than an enjoyment in dealing with sexual and other functions of the body in an ambiguous or often quite unambiguous way. One must admit, in a few instances the grotesque phantasy used in the description of these functions shows an amazing originality. But by and large, after reading the bulk of these pieces, one retains the impression that, with a very few significant exceptions, they are all alike.

Hans Rosenplüt, the earliest known author of Fastnachtspiele, wrote, if our assumptions are correct, a "Türkenfastnachtspiel."[20] The enemy of Christendom, the Sultan, appears in Nürnberg under safe conduct, and this benevolent tyrant listens to all the complaints against the estates of the realm and the various professions. In other words, the fictitious presence of this tyrant (in reality not so very benevolent) is used for a lively and not unjustified political satire.

The only other known author of Fastnachtspiele in the fifteenth century, Hans Folz, shows even stronger original traits. His ingenious use of metrical forms has been recently elucidated in a study by Hubert Heinen.[21] In a dramatization of the old Salomon and Markolf story, Folz charmingly contrasts royal sophistication and the quick-witted vulgar common sense of the peasant.[22] Time and again his other plays contain passages of a surprising directness. The cliché, so predominant in the bulk of the Fastnachtspiele, attributed to Folz, has given way to personal, individual, original dialogue. Yet the Fastnachtspiele as a whole, even those of Folz and Rosenplüt, have not freed themselves from their tradition. In spite of occasional ingenious traits and sections, they never attained the superiority that can both overcome form and traditions and yet use them and play with them. This full and real originality was only reached a hundred years later in the Fastnachtspiele of Hans Sachs.

What we said about the medieval drama may not exactly sound like a hymn of praise; however, we have not touched on the most important element in the consideration of these works. If we read the text of the Oberammergau passion play, we will most likely be dismayed by the sentimentality of the treatment, the triviality of some of the thoughts, the clumsiness of language and metric treatment, the lack of sophistication. But every time the Oberammergau play is produced, the performances are sold out; the audiences are deeply engaged, to use a modern expression. These are not just American tourists, who go to Oberammergau as they go to Heidelberg and Neuschwanstein and eat Wiener Schnitzel to fulfil some imagined cultural categorical imperative. There is no doubt a sincere experience, perhaps more religious than aesthetic, but an experience nevertheless. We have ample evidence that the religious drama of the Middle Ages had the same stirring effect. We cannot consider these pieces simply by reading their text, not even by taking text and music together, as in the liturgical drama. The play is the thing. The performance is an integral part (to repeat an often stated truism); the text is only as significant as a libretto is for an opera. Only through the performance did the texts come to life. Here was really a *Gesamtkunstwerk*, where different arts cooperated but all in subservience to the one thing, the performance. We are unable to reconstruct, to revitalize this *Gesamtkunstwerk*. It would indeed be a charming adventure to observe Benedikt Debs or Vigil Raber when they shaped their texts into a performance or Salat or Renward Cysat or even our friend Gundelfinger. We might very well then conclude that in the performances they attained what in their texts they did not attain—real originality.

NOTES

1. Karl Young, *The Drama of the Medieval Church* (Oxford, 1933), I, pp. 204-5.

2. Jude Woerdeman, "The Source of the Easter Play," *Orate Fratres* 20 (1945–46). 262–72.

3. Helmut de Boor, *Die Textgeschichte der lateinischen Osterfeiern* (Tübingen, 1967), p. 24, claims that the age of the Limoges trope is the middle of the tenth century.

4. See de Boor, but also Edith Wright, *The Dissemination of the Liturgical Drama in France* (Bryn Mawr, 1936).

5. Young, II, pp. 370–96.

6. A concise biography and bibliography: Karl Langosch, "Reichersberg, Gerhoh von," *Die deutsche Literatur des Mittelalters: Verfasserlexikon* 3 (Berlin, 1943), pp. 1022–40.

7. Young, II, pp. 463–68.

8. Wolfgang F. Michael, "Fahrendes Volk und mittelalterliches Drama," *Kleine Schriften der Gesellschaft für Theatergeschichte* 17 (1960), 3–8. See also Wolfgang F. Michael, *Frühformen der deutschen Bühne* [Schriften der Gesellschaft für Theatergeschichte 62] (Berlin, 1963), pp. 57–59.

9. Karl Ferdinand Kummer, *Erlauer Spiele* (Vienna, 1882), pp. 91–119.

10. J.E. Wackernell, *Altdeutsche Passionsspiele aus Tirol* [Quellen und Forschungen zur Geschichte, Litteratur und Sprache Österreichs1] (Graz, 1897).

11. For Lucerne, Heinz Wyss, *Das Luzerner Osterspiel* I-III (Bern, 1967).

For Donaueschingen, the edition of Franz Joseph Mone, *Schauspiele des Mittelalters* 2 (Karlsruhe, 1846) is still far better than Eduard Hartl, *Das Drama des Mittelalters* (Leipzig, 1942).

12. R. Froning, *Das Drama des Mittelalters* 2 [Deutsche National-Litteratur 14] (Stuttgart, *n.d.*).

13. The so-called Heidelberg passion, Gustav Milchsack, *Heidelberger Passionsspiel* [Bibliothek des literarischen Vereins in Stuttgart 150] (Stuttgart, 1880), was probably performed in Mainz. For Friedberg—Ernst Zimmermann, "Das Alsfelder Passionsspiel und die Wetterauer Spielgruppe," *Archiv für hessische Geschichte und Altertumskinde* n. 6 (1909): 1–206; for Fritzlar—Karl Brethauer, "Bruchstücke eines hessischen Passionsspiels," *Zeitschrift für deutsches Altertum* 68 (1931), 17–31; for Marburg—Wolfgang F. Michael, "Gab es ein Marburger Prozessionsspiel?" *Archiv für das Studium der neueren Sprachen und Literaturen* 114 (1963), 394–396; for Alsfeld—Richard Froning, *Das Drama des Mittelalters* [Deutsche National-Litteratur 14] (Stuttgart, n.d.).

14. See Wolfgang F. Michael, *Die Anfänge des Theaters zu Freiburg im Breisgau* [Zeitschirft des Freiburger Geschichtsvereins 45] (Freiburg, 1934) and *Die geistlichen Prozessionsspiele in Deutschland* [Hesperia 22] (Baltimore, 1947).

15. Friedrich Ranke, *Das Osterspiel von Muri* (Aarau, 1944).

16. Willy Krogmann, *Das Redentiner Osterspiel* [Altdeutsche Quellen 3] (Leipzig, 1937).

17. Renward Brandstetter, *Die Regenz bei den Luzerner Osterspielen* (Luzern, 1886).

18. See Adolf Reinle, "Mathias Gundelfingers Zurzacher Osterspiel von 1494 'Luzerner Grablegung,'" *Innerschweizerisches Jahrbuch für Heimatkunde* 13–14 (1949–50), 65–96.

19. Only edition: Adelbert von Keller, *Fastnachtspiele aus dem fünfzehnten Jahrhundert* 1–4 [Bibliothek des Litterarischen Vereins in Stuttgart 28-31] (Stuttgart, 1853). Best treatment: Eckehard Catholy, *Das Fastnachtspiel des Spätmittelalters* [Hermaea 8] (Tübingen, 1961). See also: Wolfgang F. Michael, *Frühformen der deutschen Bühne* [Schriften der Gesellschaft für Theatergeschichte 62] (Berlin, 1963).

20. Adelbert von Keller, *Fastnachtspiele aus dem fünfzehnten Jahrhundert* 1 [Bibliothek des Litterarischen Vereins in Stuttgart 28] (Stuttgart, 1853), pp. 288–304.

21. Hubert Heinen, *Die rhythmisch-metrische Gestaltung des Knittelverses bei Hans Folz* [Marburger Beiträge zur Germanistik 12] (Marburg, 1966).

22. Adelbert von Keller, *Fastnachtspiele aus dem fünfzehnten Jahrhundert* [Bibliothek des Litterarischen Vereins in Stuttgart 29] (Stuttgart, 1853), pp. 523–40.

THE LITERARY GENESIS OF THE LATIN
PASSION PLAY AND THE *PLANCTUS MARIAE:*
A NEW CHRISTOCENTRIC
AND MARIAN THEOLOGY

Sandro Sticca

RESEARCH on the origins and development of the medieval religious drama has been generally carried out within the confines of the evolutionary theory established by the critical method of both E.K. Chambers and Karl Young. Toward the end of his Introduction to the *Drama of the Medieval Church* Young defines his method of interpretation by asserting that the medieval drama "presents the historian a unique opportunity for isolating a literary form and observing its development from almost inarticulate origins, through centuries of earnest experiment, into firmly conceived results."[1] Young's objective and empirical method of investigation was able to account for a chronological and ever-complex development of the religious dramatic forms: from the simplest *Quem quaeritis* tropes of the ninth century to the majestic *Ludi Paschales* of the thirteenth.

His evolutionary teleology, however, was unable to convincingly establish the embryonic development of the Passion Play, and he sought, therefore, like his predecessors, to find its origins in the lyric lament known as *Planctus Mariae.* The origin of the Passion Play must be given fresh consideration, though, in the light of the discovery of a twelfth-century Latin Passion play at Montecassino,[2]

which precedes by one hundred years what scholars have traditionally considered to be the earliest extant Latin Passion Plays, the
two Latin dramas from the *Carmina Burana* collection.

The Montecassino text is not complete: it records the events of
the Passion from Judas' bargain to the Crucifixion and the *Planctus*
of the Virgin Mary. The importance of the text lies first of all in
that it is a century older than any other western Passion Play yet
known; and secondly that it allows us to complete in part an already
known fragment, the *Officium Quarti Militis*, a fourteenth-century
document of Sulmona, Italy, giving the part of a fourth soldier.

Until the Montecassino Passion was found, it had appeared safe
to observe with Young[3] and Hunningher, among others, "that
before the beginning of the thirteenth century, there is no mention
whatever of a dramatized Passion."[4] And one of the curious phenomena of literary history has been the tenacity with which modern
scholarship on the medieval drama has fostered the erroneous belief
that the two thirteenth-century Benediktbeuern Latin Passion
Plays are the earliest extant.[5] In a most recent study on the subject,
completely unaware of the existence of the Montecassino Passion,
Wilfred Werner states: "The only extensive and relatively complete
Latin Passion Plays transmitted down are the small and the large
Benediktbeuern plays."[6]

The first section of this paper will offer an investigation of the
origin of the Latin Passion Play as a literary genre and produce
evidence establishing the monastery of Montecassino as the cultural
center in which the first Latin Passion Play was written.

The recognition of the Easter and Christmas tropes as the original
germ of later Easter and Christmas liturgical plays is now unques-
tioned. Performed within the confines of Christian worship and
subservient to the end of that worship, they exhibit dramatic action
and liturgical rite in the closest conjunction. Spanning many
centuries, the plays are testimony of the growth of the liturgical
dramatic form and of the dramatic movement and temper of the
liturgy in which they find their origin.

The origin of the Latin Passion Play, however, is more doubtful
since very few Latin ones exist, and also because the full develop-

ment of vernacular Passion Plays belongs to the late Middle Ages. The distinguished scholar Karl Young had occasion to remark in his monumental opus that "in comparison with the multitude of medieval [Latin] Church plays treating events relating to the Resurrection, the number of dramatic representations of the Crucifixion is astonishingly small."[7] The Crucifixion and the events which led up to it are non-existent in the liturgical drama, for it focuses on the Resurrection and its characteristic emotion is joy. The reason for the scarcity and late appearance of these Latin dramas may be found in the fact, as Young observes, that the Mass itself offered to the medieval worshiper in visible and audible form an actual repetition of Christ's passion.[8]

The eucharistic mystery on the altar is primarily a *memoria passionis* and "particularly after the ninth century the whole Mass was explained as a comprehensive representation of the Passion of Jesus."[9] Indeed, as far back as the tenth century, Amalarius of Metz, in the preface to his *De Ecclesiasticis Officiis* wrote:

Sacramenta debent habere similitudinem aliquam earum rerum quarum sacramenta sunt. Quapropter, similis sit sacerdos Christo, sicut Panis et liquor similia sunt corpori Christi. Sic est immolatio sacerdotis in altari quodammodo ut Christi immolatio in cruce.[10]

The Mass was, indeed, conceived as an authentic drama by medieval commentators on its symbolism. Interesting and peculiar, for instance, is what Honorius of Autun writes around the year 1100:

Sciendum quod hi qui tragoedias in theatris recitabant, actus pugnantium gestibus populo repraesentabant. Sic tragicus noster pugnam Christi populo Christiano in theatro Ecclesiae gestibus suis repraesentat, eique victoriam redemptionis suae inculcat. Itaque, cum presbyter "Orate" dicit, Christum pro nobis in agonia positum exprimit, cum apostolos orare monuit.[11]

Alanus de Insulis, in the same century, comments on the historical and symbolical meaning of the Mass in the *Sermo de Cruce Domini*: "O quantum misse misterium, ubi Christi passio representatur, ubi crux Christi figuratur."[12] For the greater part of contemporary exegetes, then, already the Church is the theater, the priest is the tragic actor. The dramatic and representational tonality of the

Mass seems to have been, in part, one of the factors responsible for the late appearance of the Passion Play, for originally the people appear to have been satisfied with contemplative liturgy which possessed in itself some elements of dramaturgy. The crucifix, for instance, was a means in liturgy and literature of avoiding the necessity of realistic and immediate description, for to the faithful it was a constant and permanent expression of the meaning of the Passion. The symbolical importance of the Cross, moreover, can be perceived in the liturgical observances of Holy Week called *Adoratio Crucis, Depositio Crucis,* and *Elevatio Crucis.* Performed at Jerusalem as early as the fourth century and known to the Roman liturgy as early as the eighth, the *Adoratio* took place on Good Friday with both the clergy and the congregation adoring and later kissing the Cross. The *Depositio* and the *Elevatio* ceremonies, symbolizing the Burial and Resurrection, took place respectively on Good Friday and Easter morning before Matins. These latter ceremonies seem to have been attached to the *Adoratio* as a kind of progression.

Although lacking genuine dramatic elements, these ceremonies exhibit unmistakably vivid attempts at some sort of representation commemorating several of the events of Christ's Passion. They cannot be considered, however, as the religious source from which a drama of the Passion stemmed.[13] Nor can its formation be found, as Young at first firmly and later cautiously suggested, in the singing of the *Passio* during Holy Week.[14] Although the singing of the *Passio* with the distribution of the principal parts was primarily instituted to dramatize the Gospel narrative,[15] this ceremony cannot be considered true drama, nor can it have had any influence on the origin of the Latin Passion Play. As to the theory that the *Planctus* must be looked upon as the germinal point of the Latin Passion, I will show later in the paper that the *Planctus* is a simple lyric expression, essentially nondramatic.

The literary genesis of the Latin Passion Play must be sought in a shift in emphasis which took place in art and literature. The realization of the first Latin Passion was made possible by general artistic and cultural changes which, starting in early Christian art, liturgy and literature, reached their climax in the eleventh and twelfth centuries. The new manifestations brought about a growing interest in and concentration on Christocentric piety, which found its greatest expression in an increased dwelling on the subject of the Passion. In art the shift is manifested by a more humanistic treatment of Christ and in literature by a consideration of the scenes of the Passion as dramatic human episodes. In both, the change is from a contemplative to a more vivid visual experience.

It would be impossible, I think, and unprofitable to present all available evidence of that liturgical, artistic and literary activity, which from the earliest centuries of the Christian era, centered on the Passion. It suffices to point out, however, that although serious attempts at rendering a faithful account of Christ's Passion appear in the fourth, fifth and sixth centuries, they lack sensitive human accents. Iconography and liturgy are primarily interested in celebrating the *Verbum*, the triumphant Divinity, the source of life and salvation; in literature, such works as Ambrose's *De Passione Domini*, Sedulius' *A solis ortus cardine* and Fortunatus' *Vexilla regis prodeunt* celebrate ontologically the atemporal and eternal meaning of the Passion, they celebrate Christ *in sancta cruce* rather than *in parasceve*, their theme was not the Passion, but the stupendous triumph: *Pange lingua gloriosi proelium certaminis*.

From the tenth century on, however, Christ's passion acquired a continuous and ever-increasing popularity as one of the favorite sacred mysteries, until within the general framework of Christian worship, by chance and coincidence, new forces were produced in Southern Italy which allowed a more eloquent and humane visualization and description of Christ's anguish in his Passion. Thus was laid the foundation of a religious *Zeitgeist* which could permit the creation, early in the twelfth century, of the first Latin Passion Play in the monastery of Montecassino.

The new forces at work are the mystical concentration on Christ's human suffering as articulated primarily by St. Anselm and St. Bernard, the Romanesque revival of the eleventh century which introduced a fresh interest in humanism, and the Byzantine school of miniature and painting in Southern Italy.

In *The Making of the Middle Ages* R.W. Southern recognizes the value of these new attitudes by remarking that "the theme of tenderness and compassion for the sufferings and helplessness of the Saviour of the world was one which had a new birth in the monasteries of the eleventh century."[16] Some scholars find the heralds of this Christocentric piety early in that century in monastic figures such as St. William of Volpiano (d. 1031), St. Richard of Verdun (d. 1046), and especially Volpiano's nephew and favorite disciple, John of Fécamp (d. 1078).

It was left, however, to St. Anselm (1033-1109) to supply the theological and theoretical justification for Christ's sufferings through a new interpretation of the necessity of the Redemption. In the *Cur Deus Homo*, a Christological treatise reminiscent of those of the second to fifth centuries, St. Anselm emphasizes the true significance of the humanity of Christ by stressing the fact that the redemptive act took place on a human level. St. Anselm felt that although a God with superhuman strength, Christ did acquire human flesh and did suffer as a human being. He carried out mankind's redemption *quasi homo*, and His divinity did not imply the least limitation of His humanity. Honorius of Autun echoes typical medieval exegesis when he states that, although Christ's nature is divine and eternal, *in humanitate habuit initium nascendo, finem moriendo*. The doctrine of the Incarnation and its implication for the salvation of man was, during the Middle Ages, as fundamental a theological tenet as the belief that Christ suffered as a man. The mystic literature of the twelfth century, in particular that of the Victorine school, was fond of pointing out the *sublimitas* and *humilitas* of the God-Man, especially in Christ's Incarnation and Passion, which realize the two most perfectly.

The devotion to Christ's Passion, which stirred the souls of pious monks early in the eleventh century and was fostered in the same generation by the delicate sensibility of St. Anselm, finds its most profound expression in the concentrated pathos devoted to it by St. Bernard (1091-1153). An unremitting love for Jesus crucified was the focal point of St. Bernard's life and the guide for his interior feelings and emotions: "haec mea sublimior interim philosophia, scire Jesum, et hunc crucifixum."[17] St. Bernard's treatment of Christ's suffering founded a new strain of spirituality for his writings "dès le XIIe siècle, orientèrent les cœurs vers les mystères de la vie terrestre, en particulier vers ceux de sa naissance et de sa passion."[18] There can be no doubt that mystical contemplation of the doctrine of the Incarnation must have contributed to arouse the desire to represent the Passion dramatically. The Christocentric mysticism of St. Anselm and St. Bernard soon acquired a religious universality by being incorporated into the common body of Christian opinion. By virtue of their example and personal reputation —St. Anselm as the Primate of England and the so-called Father of Scholasticism, St. Bernard as the renowned *doctor mellifluus*, the founder of the Cistercians, the preacher of the Second Crusade— and both through the efforts of their pupils and monastic orders which fostered the perpetuity of their teachings, medieval spirituality came to know Christ with a more delicate intimacy and dwelt primarily on his Passion.

This general shift towards a realistic depiction of the Passion is not peculiar to literature but can be traced and observed in the visual arts too. We had occasion to point out earlier how the Romanesque revival of the eleventh century, with its preference for emotional rather than intellectual apprehension of dogma, had produced a fresh interest in humanism; one of its first results, religiously, was a new trend in the iconography of Christ on the Cross. Up to this time Christ had rarely been represented dead on the Cross.[19] From the fifth century to the beginning of the eleventh the prevalent type of the Crucified, in Europe, is the *Christus triumphans*, the Pantocrator, Lord and Master of the Universe. This type shows Christ alive on the Cross, with his eyes open, the body erect and without signs of pains to indicate the triumphant and divine qualities of Christ. The attempt is always to transcend the real, to negate the value of the transcient, to deny the natural and earthly in its evocation of permanent values.

Although such early iconographical monuments as the Rabula crucifixion of 586 exhibit an inclination toward a more dramatic and humanizing representation of Christ on the Cross, and although

45

the substitution of the figure of Christ for that of the Lamb in crucifixion scenes was decreed by the council *in Trullo* of Constantinople
in the year 692 for the avowed purpose of emphasizing the humanity
of the theological mystery, the figure of the Crucified remained
devoid of realistic details and followed even throughout the Carolingian artistic revival the compositional laws of early hieratic
iconography.

From the eleventh century on it is a second type of the Crucified,
however, expressing suffering and human nature, which becomes
increasingly common and with one important difference: Christ
is represented now dead on the Cross, eyes closed, head lowered,
the body slightly bent in a rhythmic curve, and blood and water
issuing from his wounded side.[20] Art too appears to be exploiting
and conveying the deep emotion which Christ's sacrifice had, at
this time, aroused. The peculiar feature of this art is its preoccu-
pation with the tangible and immediate rather than with the
symbolical and theological—a desire to embrace and express the
divine by emphasizing the actual and the concrete. The dramatic
potentialities suggested by this new iconography of the Crucified
in the formulation of a Latin Passion in Southern Italy will become
readily apparent when one considers that, although sporadic representations of Christ dead on the Cross appear, in Europe, as
early as the eighth century, this type was unfamiliar in Italy as late
as the first half of the eleventh century[21] and was introduced there
in the same century by way of Byzantine influence.

This influence was made possible, in part, by the close rela-
tions existing for centuries between Montecassino and Byzantium,
and by the fact that geographically, politically and racially the
south of Italy has been comparatively isolated from the rest of the
peninsula. The most conspicuous time of Byzantine influence,
however, begins in the eleventh century, when the Beneventan
noble Desiderius, who later became Pope Victor III, was elected
abbot (1058-1086) of Montecassino. One of Desiderius' first acts
was to set about the reconstruction of the entire monastery, and
especially the basilica of St. Benedict. To this end, he not only
ordered and imported works of art from Constantinople but sum-

moned Greek craftsmen skilled in mosaic, metal works, and illumination of manuscripts.

The most characteristic activity developed at Cassino under the stimulating influence of Byzantine artists is the art of illumination. It is under Desiderius that Montecassino became one of the chief centers for the production of South Italian manuscripts, particularly the *Exultet Rolls*,[22] which in the liturgy of the Roman Church were used in the ceremony of the blessing of the Paschal Candle on Easter Eve. Inscribed on a long strip of parchment or vellum, the text of the *Exultet Roll* was annotated with musical neumes and illustrated with illuminated pictures. The peculiar feature of the roll is that the pictures are in reverse to the text. As the deacon chanted and unrolled the scroll, the illustrations of the unrolled portion he had just read, would fall over the back of the ambo before him, thus displaying them right side up to the congregation.

The distinctive value of these rolls lies in their liturgical use, for "the principal purpose of these rolls was to obtain in the religious ceremony a more complete comprehension and participation on the part of the faithful."[23] The dramatic aspects of the *Exultet* rolls cannot be questioned since the people, as spectators, were given a vivid representation in tableaux, in a kind of cinematic sequence, of some of the most memorable events in Christ's life from his birth and ministry to his Passion and Resurrection.

The influence of Byzantine iconography is perceptible everywhere in Southern Italy, particularly in the frescoes which, from the eleventh to the thirteenth centuries, appeared on the walls of its churches. Of particular interest are the Byzantine frescoes appearing on the walls of the south Italian church of St. Angelo in Formis, which was presented to Desiderius in 1072 by Richard, Prince of Capua. Here the sequences of New Testament paintings which decorate the central nave reproduce the events leadings to the Passion of Christ with scrupulous fidelity. The paintings show unusual attention to the dramatic and the pathetic, as can be gathered from the violent scene of Judas' betrayal and the sorrow and tears on the face of the Virgin and the Holy Women at the Crucifixion. The historical significance of the entire cycle of frescoes of St. Angelo in Formis in understanding medieval spirituality at Montecassino cannot be emphasized enough.

The decorations on the walls of St. Angelo in Formis, many of which bear underneath appropriate Latin phrases, must be seen in strict analogy with Desiderius' method of decorations used in the basilica of Montecassino. The method of decorating the text with suitable pictures is conspicuous at this time in all the artistic productions associated with the Montecassino renaissance of the eleventh and twelfth centuries, whether it be, as we have seen, the illumination of the *Exultet Rolls* and other manuscripts, the beautification of church walls, or, later on, the illumination with Passion scenes of the very text on which the first Latin Passion was written.

Although Passion cycles were known to the southern Italian monastic communities from the seventh century,[24] none of them can be compared in faithfulness to the gospel account and in fullness of details to the great Gospel and Passion cycles of the eleventh century introduced into Southern Italy through Byzantine influence. The Passion frescoes of St. Angelo in Formis, in their actual unfolding of events in a series of pictorial representations, constitute a progressive narrative, an attempt to present the Bible story as a staged drama, in a basically theatrical form. It is for these reasons that Paul Weber, in 1894, with historical and literary foresight could describe the frescoes of St. Angelo in Formis as "the first painted representation of a medieval Passion Play" and point out its importance for the history of the religious drama by remarking: "This is a phenomenon which research on the religious drama should from now on take into consideration."[25]

The purpose of this last discussion has not been to overemphasize the importance of the Passion frescoes of St. Angelo in Formis but rather to indicate that, through Byzantine influence, at Montecassino and within its religious domain, artistic forces were at work which, coupled with mystical and literary trends and attitudes towards a deeper interest in Christ's suffering and Passion, and with the general artistic revival inaugurated by abbot Desiderius in all the arts, produced a milieu in which the first Latin Passion, early in the twelfth century, could originate. When one considers that the religious plays are essentially the products of the main-stream of medieval thought rather than sporadic and isolated examples of drama *per se*, when one considers that whether in art, in literature or mystical ideas, monastic residents of Montecassino saw the same Christocentric attitude, it is not surprising if a competent monk should have decided to express those very attitudes in a dramatic form. The twelfth-century Montecassino Latin Passion Play bears witness to the fact that indeed he did.

* * *

Virtually all the earlier historians of the medieval religious drama have regarded the *Planctus Mariae* as the most influential factor in dictating the emergence of a drama of the Passion. As early as 1893, the German scholar Wechssler states in the *Die Romanischen Marienklagen* that the early Middle Ages knew no other dramatization of Christ's Passion outside of the *Planctus Mariae*.[26] The same idea was expressed by the French scholar De Julleville and the German Creizenach.

A more reserved opinion was expressed by George Coffin Taylor, one of the first English scholars to study the *Planctus*. While recognizing that the theory regarding the *Planctus* as the germ of the Passion play does not seem to apply to such late compositions as the English plays, Taylor felt that it could apply to an early period of the drama.[27] Among more recent scholars of the medieval religious drama, Karl Young concluded, after giving a brilliant examination of the *Planctus*, that "so far as we can tell, the composition of the *Planctus Mariae* was the first step taken towards the dramatization of the Passion."[28] Young's conclusion stems from his theory, shared also by contemporary medieval scholars, that the use of the *Planctus Mariae* in the drama may have been suggested to ecclesiastical poets by older laments, such as those uttered by the three Marys and such separate twelfth-century laments of the Virgin as Geoffrey of Breteuil's *Planctus ante nescia*, and a highly dramatic thirteenth-century *Planctus* beginning: *Flete fideles animae*.[29] More recently, a German scholar, Richard Kienast, in "Die Deutschsprachige Lyrik des Mittelalters," contributes to this

49

polarization of ideas by indicating that the laments of Mary are a lyric subspecies in Latin church poetry that later evolved into dramatic form. These *Planctus* which, according to Lipphardt[30] and Kienast,[31] were originally sung on Good Friday, were sometimes transformed into semidramatic representations:

In the beginning their form was lyric; but soon the dialogue kernels developed. And with the delineation of the action, from the hymn one passed into drama, which gave shape to the representation of the attitudes of the *Virgo dolens* and of the Marys present with her at the foot of the Cross, with a realistic development and an elaborate amplification of the scene hardly alluded to in the Gospel.[32]

The highly dramatic fourteenth-century *Planctus* preserved at Cividale,[33] Italy, for instance, with its many rubrics prescribing gestures for the actors, has some nine of the speeches which are also found, in large part, in the lyric *Planctus* "Flete fideles animae."[34] To heighten the dramatic moment, later *Planctus* redactors would indiscriminately incorporate stanzas from earlier ones, concerned less with thematic unity than with pathos. One of the two recently discovered fourteenth-century Latin *Planctus* in the *Biblioteca Civica* of Bergamo,[35] Italy, exhibits three stanzas from the "Flete fideles animae" *Planctus* and two from an undated *Planctus* beginning "Qui per viam pergitis."[36] A third fourteenth-century *Planctus* found in the *Ordinarium Ecclesiae Patavinae*[37] of the Biblioteca Capitolare of Padova, Italy, has some twelve stanzas from the "Flete fideles animae" *Planctus*.

On the whole, the reasoning of Young and Kienast is the same as that of Creizenach, who asserted that the dialogue amplifications of the Sequence of the Good Friday liturgy were transformed into drama at a time when there were no true Passion Plays, and that the writers of Passion Plays employed them later for their dramatic purposes.[38]

I now come to the original part of my study on the *Planctus*. Although various arguments have been presented to suggest a possible derivation of the Passion Play from the *Planctus*, up to now no real evidence has been offered to prove the origin of a Passion Play in a *Planctus*. Even the Cividale, Bergamo and Padova laments, though full of realistic movements which approach true drama, do not represent events which precede and follow the Crucifixion itself.

Possibly, as some scholars have suggested, the *Planctus* may be taken into account as one element of development, though not as the formative starting point of the Passion drama.[39] In this respect, I agree with the theatrical critic Hardin Craig, who wisely observes that "although these *Planctus* are always found in Passion plays, they are not in essence dramatic and are not the seed from which the Passion grew."[40] I agree to this but not for the reason given. In an article entitled "The Origin of the Passion Play: Matters of Theory as Well as Fact," Craig observes that in order to be dramatic a piece of writing must have action, impersonation, and dialogue, the *sine qua non* of a drama, and adds that this is hardly true of the *Planctus*, for they lack action.[41]

On the contrary, a *Planctus* as included in a play may indeed be dramatic by adding movement and providing a lyric intensification of the dramatic moment. My primary support is the twelfth-century Montecassino Passion Play. It contains at the end a very brief *Planctus* which presents just the three things which are considered by Craig to be the *sine qua non* of a drama: action, impersonation and dialogue. Indeed, in our Passion the Virgin is described crying with gestures at the foot of the Cross while she recites a three-line vernacular lament:

> ...te portai nillu meu ventre
> Quando te beio [mo] ro presente
> Nillu teu regnu agi me a mmente.[42]

But let us return to Young's discussion for a moment. The fundamental reasoning upon which he and his successors base their theory of the origin of the Passion Play from the *Planctus* is the following: that some of the laments are dramatic, and that the *Planctus ante nescia*, which appears in many plays of the thirteenth century, goes back actually to the twelfth century.[43]

Any weight given this time sequence, even in the weak form of a *post hoc, ergo propter hoc*, can now be dispensed with, since the Montecassino play presents a twelfth-century Passion more dramatic and more extensive than any extant formal laments of the twelfth or thirteenth century and contains at the end a very brief *Planctus* which is as early as the extended lyric *Planctus ante nescia*, if not earlier. The theory, then, that the *Planctus* is the germinal point of the Passion Plays falls to pieces, for, since we now have a text of the Passion, anterior or at least contemporary to the *Planctus*, this comes to lose its importance as the creative element of the Passion.

Moreover, there seems to be no theoretical reason why the *Planctus* should be supposed to be earlier than the representation of the Passion itself; for, after all, to the faithful the most important liturgical fact to be remembered during Lent was not Mary's lament, but Christ's Passion. The lament of the Virgin was an incidental element in Christ's Passion, and not vice versa. For, as Emile Mâle tells us, "the Passion was in fact the one subject of compelling interest to men of the Middle Ages."[44]

The Church gave emphasis to the Easter liturgy, for the consecration and sanctification of Christ accomplished in the resurrection affected all men, and the Christian's ultimate stage of perfection is attained with his bodily resurrection in Christ: *Pascha nostrum immolatus est Christus ... Qui mortem nostram moriendo destruxit, et vitam resurgendo reparavit.*[45] (Christ our Pasch was sacrificed...who by dying has destroyed death in us, and by rising has restored life).

It is true, as Young suggests, that meditations on Mary's suffering appear early in the Western Church, but it is also true that these meditations always appear in connection with the Passion of Jesus. Even in such treatises on Mary's sufferings as the twelfth-century *Liber de Passione* of Bernard,[46] Anselm's *Dialogus Mariae et Anselmi de Passione Domini*,[47] the thirteenth-century *Stabat Mater* of Jacopone da Todi[48] (1230 - 1306) and the fourteenth-century Pseudo-Bonaventure's *Meditationes Vitae Christi*,[49] the Passion of Christ is always the predominant consideration. In Bernard's *Liber de Passione*, for instance, we are struck by the feelings given to Mary:

Aspiciebat et ipse benignissimo vultu me matrem plorantem, et me verbis paucis consolari voluit. Sed ipsis consolari non poteram, sed flebam dicendo, et dicebam plorando: Fili mi, quis mihi dabit, ut ego moriar pro te? Moritur filius, cur nec secum misera moritur mater ejus? Amor unice, fili me dulcissime, noli me derelinquere post te, trade me ad te ipsum, ut ipsa moriar tecum.[50]

But in his *Meditatio in Passionem et Resurrectionem Domini*, in the *Lamentatio in Passionem Christi*, in the *Sermo de Vita et Passione Domini*,[51] it is to Jesus' Passion that he gives prominence. And in his *Rhythmica Oratio ad unum quodlibet membrorum Christi patientis et Cruce pendentis*, he pours forth a lament which must be considered one of the noblest outbursts of compassion to come out of a human heart:

AD PEDES

Plagas tuas rubicundas,
Et fixuras tam profundas,
Cordi meo fac inscribi,
Ut configar totus tibi,
Te modis amans omnibus....

AD MANUS

In hac cruce sic intensus,
In te meos trahe sensus,
Meum posse, velle, scire,
Cruci tuae fac servire...

AD FACIEM

Salve, caput cruentatum,
Totum spinis coronatum,
Conquassatum, vulneratum,
Arundine verberatum,
Facie sputie illita.

In hac tua passione,
Me agnosce, Pastor bone...

Non me reum asperneris,
Nec indignum dedigneris,
Morte tibi jam vicina,
Tuum caput hic inclina,
In meis pausa brachiis.

Tuae sanctae passioni
Me gauderem interponi,
In hac cruce tecum mori;
Praesta crucis amatori
Sub cruce tua moriar.[52]

53

In the thirteenth century, also, Saint Bonaventure is mainly concerned with considerations upon the life and Passion of Jesus in the *Lignum Vitae*, in the *Officium de Passione*, in the *Vitis mystica* and elsewhere. In the *De Perfectione Vitae*, he writes, for instance, "Quoniam devotionis fervor per frequentem Christi passionis memoriam nutritur et conservatur in homine, ideo necesse est, ut frequenter, ut semper oculis cordis sui Christum in cruce tamquam morientem videat qui devotionem in se vult inextinguibilem conservare."[53] This lingering on the Passion of Christ was a duty for the Christian and especially for the Franciscan, for whom the whole of religious experience was summed up in the motto of the Order: "Mihi absit gloriari nisi in cruce Domini."[54] Participation in Christ's Passion was a cherished ideal for St. Francis[55] and indeed the sufferings of the Redeemer upon the Cross are for Bonaventure as for every Franciscan "the center of all man's hope of salvation, his only consolation, his sorrow and his delight."[56] This profound concern for Christ's suffering and the pathos its meditations evoked can be best observed in a few stanzas from Bonaventure's *Laudismus de Sancta Cruce*.[57] Here the faithful are invited to remember Christ's Passion, to meditate upon it, to delight in it:

> Recordare sanctae crucis,
> Qui perfectam vitam ducis,
>   Delectare iugiter;
> Sanctae crucis recordare,
> Et in ipsa meditare
>   Insatiabiliter.

And as if this were not enough, the faithful are invited to live in the light of the Cross and actually grow with it:

> Stes in cruce Christo duce,
> Donec vivas in hac luce
>   Moto procul taedio,
> Non quiescas nec tepescas,
> In hac crescas et calescas
>   Cordis desiderio.

And finally, after an intense meditation and elaboration on the theological and symbolical grandeur of the Cross, the final mystical sublimation is attained in a direct relation between the faithful and the Cross:

> Hoc est opus salutare
> Circa crucem laborare
> Corde, ore, opere.[58]

It seems to me evident, then, that meditations upon the Passion of Christ in the twelfth and thirteenth centuries are coeval with meditations upon the sufferings of Mary.

The temporal coexistence of this Christian and Marian piety can be best explained in terms of the religious *Zeitgeist* of the twelfth century which made possible their parallel development. Mystical concentration on Christ's human suffering and on Mary's compassion for her Son are indeed most intensely felt in that century. And just as the stimulus towards a representation of a Passion Play was supplied by a consideration of Christ's human nature in the redemptive act, so too it is possible to trace the antecedents of the *Planctus Mariae* in terms of the theological discussions pertaining to Mary's role in the redemption of man. Nowhere in the Bible are expressions of grief attributed to the Virgin Mary. Of the four Gospel writers only John records her presence at the Crucifixion. Yet this episode was to receive particular attention from the medieval dramatists. They were fascinated with the dramatic possibilities inherent in Mary's behavior at the foot of the Cross and invariably gave prominence to her maternal sorrow at the sight of her suffering Son. In this they preferred to follow tradition. Early Fathers and theologians, while recognizing the fact that the Virgin did suffer in Calvary, differed widely on the question of her behavior. On the basis of John's account, "Stabant autem iuxta crucem Iesu mater eius, et soror matris eius, Maria Cleophae, et Maria Magdalene," St. Ambrose wrote: "Stabat Sancta Maria iuxta crucem filii et spectabat virgo sui unigeniti passionem; stantem illam lego, flentem non lego."[58]

The vision of an austere and ascetic Virgin seems to have been prevalent in the early years of the Christian era. Her steadfastness at the Crucifixion is commented upon in an Ambrosian *Missale*, for instance, in the preface to the feast of Mary's seven sorrows.[59]

Writing on the subject, in an article entitled "Studien zu den Marienklagen und Germanische Totenklage," Professor Lipphardt remarks that "dem ganzen frühen Mittelalter galt Maria unter dem Kreuz als das Vorbild für alle, die einen lieben toten zu betrauern hatten. Wie sie durch Christus gestärkt worden war, so sollten sich alle christen nach ihrem Beispiele verhalten und in der Trauer standhaft bleiben."[60] The Church Fathers, in particular, suggested that Mary was aware of the mystery of Redemption, and consequently endured her Son's death for the salvation of mankind. It is for this reason that in the West, during the first ten centuries, there are no extended Latin meditations upon the sorrows of the Virgin.

A different tradition, however, particularly in the Eastern Church, emphasized Mary's maternal instinct and tears. Indeed, the oldest lamentation of the Virgin as a liturgical motif is contained in the apocryphal Greek Gesta Pilati B, dated no later than the fifth century.[61] Here it is related how the Virgin fell unconscious on the way to the Golgotha and wept in despair at the Cross. It is, however, through a chronological analysis of the Marian exegetical tradition that one comes to realize the theological shift in attitudes which brought about the humanizing of the Virgin's suffering at the foot of the Cross. In the earliest days of the Church Mary's chief attribute was her human nature, for the Church was eager to stress the reality of the Incarnation. During the Patristic period, however, efforts are made to more clearly define the role of the Virgin in the redemptive mystery. Beginning with Justin in the middle of the second century, Mary is presented as the new Eve, a parallel which corresponds in outline to that between Christ and Adam, for, just as Eve, by her disobedience, brought death upon the human race, so Mary, by her obedience, brought salvation. Eve's effort resulted in death and Mary's in deliverance from death.[62] The Mary-Eve parallel was further developed by Iranaeus who delved into the ethical aspects of man's redemption by indicating that Eve's influence in producing man's sinful condition was paralleled by Mary's influence in freeing him from this condition.[63] The Mary-Eve parallel did not undergo a significant development after the third century, but it was frequently repeated. Tertullian, for instance, emphasizes the contrast between the two women in terms of Mary's faith in God and Eve's trust in Satan.[64] St. Ambrose, who contrasted the two women more generally on the basis of virginity, called Mary the Mother of salvation in contrast to Eve, the Mother of the race.[65] St. Jerome in his typically deft style states: "Death through Eve, life through Mary."[66] This theme was constantly repeated through the patristic age. Particularly after the Council of Ephesus (A.D. 431), which pronounced her Mother of God (Theotokos), the West gives stress to Mary's grandeur and the influence she exercised, by virtue of her maternal authority, over her omnipotent Son. And it is in the fifth century that the mother of Christ receives liturgical recognition for the first time, a recognition which is concerned primarily with her lofty and exalted dignity rather than her maternal and human nature.

Exalted above the angels and saints of Heaven, referred to in her coredemptive association with Christ as the Second Eve, identified with *Mater Ecclesia*, soon she came to be regarded as the mediatrix of all graces, the suppliant intercessor before the throne of God. Paul the Deacon in the eighth century is the first to refer to her as *"mediatrix Dei ad homines."*[67] Although the flowering of the mediatorial role of the Virgin can be first observed during the eleventh century in the hymnological, homiletic and sequential compositions—by such as Fulbert of Chartres (d. 1029), Bernon of Reichnau (d. 1048), Odilon of Cluny (d. 1049), Saint Peter Damian (d. 1072), St. Anselm of Lucca (d. 1086), Cardinal Alberic of Montecassino (d. 1088), Radbod of Noyon (d. 1098),[68] it is primarily in the twelfth century, at Citaux, within the confines of Benedictine monasticism that one finds the full blossoming and theological crystallization of Mary's mediation. Monastic figures such as Serlon of Savigny (d. 1148), Guerric of Igny (d. 1151), Aelred of Rievaulx (d. 1167), Nicholas of Clairvaux (d. 1176), Alanus of Lille (d. 1202), compose for the Virgin sermons which not only comment on all the mysteries of the Redemption but particularly on her universal mediation.[69] It is St. Anselm of Canterbury, however, who defines the main features of this mediation by pointing out that Mary is the gate of life and the door of salvation for all:

Mater restitutionis omnium. St. Anselm not only establishes a parallel between the fatherhood of God and the motherhood of Mary but also gives greater stress, in the Incarnation, to the Motherhood of Mary than to the condescension of the Logos. And he even goes so far as to assert that both damnation and salvation depend on Christ's as well as Mary's will.[70] St. Bernard, on the other hand, while recognizing that Christ is the true Mediator, stresses the necessity of Mary's mediation, for men fear Christ their Judge and need, therefore, a "mediator with that Mediator," for Mary is sweet and gentle and unable to judge any.[71] It is important to observe in this respect that Mary's mediation assumes for St. Bernard a theocentric aspect, since it is specifically stated that Mary's mediation is in accord with the divine intention.

Mary's humanity, however, came to be more generally associated with her earthly suffering, clearest image of her humility, and a more proximate cooperation of Mary in the redemptive act is linked with her motherhood. Mary's role is not sacrificial in the strict sense that Christ's is but "Mary's interior dispositions, characterized as Christ's were by universal love and perfect obedience to the Father, were perfectly oriented to sacrifice and enabled her to share in her own way in Christ's offering of himself."[72] Arnauld of Bonnevalle writes, for instance, in the twelfth century:

Dividunt coram Patre inter se mater et Filius pietatis officia, et miris allegationibus muniunt redemptionis humanae negotium, et conducunt inter se reconciliationis nostrae inviolabile testamentum.[73]

In considering Christ's sacrifice as a liturgical action, Arnauld comes also to suggest the idea of Mary's priesthood. Mary is an associate in the work of redemption because she is also an associate in the mystery of the Incarnation. But in Mary's motherhood contemporary exegetes chose to emphasize her vulnerability to human suffering, to tears, to sorrow.

As a consequence, just as the initial impetus to the production of a Passion Play was supplied by the intense Christocentric mysticism of the eleventh and twelfth centuries, so too the embryonic nucleus in the redaction of the *Planctus Mariae* sprang out of the meditations on the sorrows of Mary which, beginning in the eleventh century, reach their climax in the twelfth, and by virtue of their pathetic commentary on the sacrifice on the Cross show the natural ties that exist between the *Passio* and the *Compassio*. Although Patristic writings had generally commented on Mary's instrumentality in the Passion by indicating that she cooperated proximately, directly, and immediately in the achievement of the redemption, eleventh- and twelfth-century commentaries emphasized her sorrows and human agony, seeing in the Virgin the figure of the *Mater dolorosa* experiencing in her heart Christ's suffering.

The theory of the Zeitgeist will seem even more plausible since it is precisely the twelfth century that shines as the period of richest development in the formulation of a kind of *liturgie mariale* which finds its highest expression in the hyperdulia given the Virgin.[74] More than at any other period Mary became the object of fervent veneration, and numerous devotional practices sprang up in her honor.[75]

In view of the pietistic attitudes which I have illustrated, it seems quite anachronistic on the part of scholars such as Mâle to state that "de même que l'on dit *Christi Passio* on commence à dire dès le XIVᵉ siècle, *Mariae Compassio*."[76] This is hardly true. To be sure, pathetic expressions on Mary's sorrows are more frequent in the thirteenth and fourteenth centuries, but the theme of the *Compassio* began in the eleventh century,[77] flourished in the twelfth,[78] and found its most intense lyric effusion in the thirteenth with the stream of Franciscan piety: St. Bonaventure, Peckam, and Jacopone da Todi.

Peter Damiani (988-1072), commenting on the prophecy of Simeon, appears to be the first to have introduced the term *Compassio* in the sense which will be predominant in later centuries:

Et tuam ipsius animan pertransivit gladius. Ac si diceret: dum Filius tuus senserit passionem in corpore, te etiam transfiget *gladius compassionis* in mente.[79]

But it is with St. Anselm of Canterbury in the eleventh and St. Bernard in the twelfth century that comes into being the triumphant period of meditation on the suffering and compassion of the Virgin at the foot of the Cross. St. Anselm by virtue of his famous *Dialogus Mariae et Anselmi de Passione Domini*[80] and more particularly through the *Oratio XX*,[81] St. Bernard by the *Liber de Passione Christi et Doloribus et Planctibus Matris Eius*,[82] introduced Christianity to a new current of piety emphasizing Mary's maternal sorrow and compassion. A piety which rendered intelligible and human the relationship between Mother and Son, became later of inestimable importance in the redaction of vernacular Passion plays, and readily assumed prominence in contemporary monastic writings.

John of Fécamp, for instance, one of the most intense Christocentric mystics and contemporary of St. Anselm, in his prayer "Ardens Desiderium ad Christum" comments thus on Mary's compassion: "Cur, o anima mea, non es compassa sanctissimae Matri eius, dilectae Domine meae, cum ineffabilibus singultibus Unigeniti sui dilectissimi membra coram se cruci confixa vehementissime defleret"[83] St. Anselm of Lucca states that Mary "non potuit sine incomparabili dolore uidere in crucis patibulo gloriosissimum filium clavis affixum."[84] Arnauld of Bonnevalle, in the twelfth century, stressing the co-immolation of Christ and Mary, writes: "Quod in carne Christi agebant clavi et lancea, hoc in ejus [Mariae] mente compassio naturalis et affectionis maternae angustia."[85] Eadmer, the most famous of Anselm's English disciples, elaborating on Mary's sorrow in the *De Compassione beatae Mariae pro filio crucifixo*, says: "Vere pertransivit animam tuam gladius doloris, qui tibi amarior exstitit omnibus doloribus cujusvis passionis corporeae."[86] Richard of St. Victor emphasizing Mary's more immediate cooperation in man's salvation, states: "sicut non fuit amor sicut amor ejus, ita non fuit dolor similis dolori ejus."[87] It is in Bernard's mysticism, however, that the theme of the compassion acquires a deep-rooted human and personal treatment. Commenting on Mary's compassion within the context of her mediatorial and redemptive role, St. Bernard calls it a *martyrium cordis* and indicates that undoubtedly Mary's inner sorrow over Christ's corporeal passion was exceeded by the intensity of her compassion: "in qua [Maria] nimirum corporeae sensum passionis excesserit compassionis effectus."[88]

The development of the theme of the *Compassio* in the eleventh and twelfth centuries was also aided and fostered by a definite shift of attitudes in the artistic portrayals of Christ. As we have seen, beginning in the eleventh century, the representation of Christ dead on the Cross—accentuating with poignant realism the "vir dolorum et sciens humanitatem"—created another stimulus towards artistic and meditative portrayals of the Virgin sorrowing at the foot of the Cross. Some of the most lyrical of the meditations on Mary's sorrow and *Compassio* were, in the twelfth century, incorporated in and absorbed by *Planctus* such as the famous twelfth-century *Planctus ante nescia*.[89] This was made possible by the fact that at that time terms such as *Compassio, Planctus, Lamentatio,* and *Transfixio* had the same meaning. Later these *Planctus* were incorporated, with little or no change, into dramas as independent lyric compositions. It would appear, then, that the common occurrences of the *Planctus* as a theme in the religious poetry and meditations of the day is evidence that it is just one manifestation of the extensive cult of the Virgin in the twelfth century.[90]

We may safely conjecture, then, that when a twelfth-century cleric or monk had drafted a play on the Passion of Christ, he might also incorporate in it a lament of the Virgin in order to heighten the poignancy of the Crucifixion scene. This possibility is strengthened by the consideration of the relatively small importance of the *Planctus* in various plays and by the fact that the earliest extant Passion of Montecassino and the two thirteenth-century Benediktbeuern Passion Plays from Germany present together the Passion and some sort of *Planctus*.

Later, however, with the fuller development of both play and lyric, the expression of a grief without comfort goes on freeing itself from the sensational encumbrance of the traditional apparatus of the Passion; the multitude of Jews, the soldiers, the thieves, in short the spectacle of the crowd which in the phantasmagoria of the Passion was able to neglect and sometimes to forget completely the humanity of the religious sentiment.[91]

Indeed, although the commemoration of Jesus' Passion remained

61

always the most solemn and stirring moment of the dramatic representation, slowly the people's imagination became increasingly fascinated with the more human suffering at the Golgotha, a mother's for her Son. Realizing that the vision of the grieving figure of the *Virgo moerens* was able to generate a more intense participation of the people in the representation of Jesus' Passion, later medieval dramatists heightened the pathos of that scene by elaborating on available Latin sequences on Mary's maternal grief and by creating new ones. It is in this manner that long, dramatic *Planctus* such as the fourteenth-century Cividale one were produced.[92]

Particularly in England, at this time, the motif of the lamenting mother becomes the subject of forceful sermons[93] and one of the highlights of a number of religious poems written at the close of the thirteenth and beginning of the fourteenth century, the oldest appearing in *The Assumption of Our Lady*. From the Cursor Mundi to the *Northern Passion*, from the *Southern Passion* to *A Stanzaic Life of Christ*, one witnesses the popularity of the Mother's supreme expression of love and compassion for the Son. Equally important is the role assigned the Virgin in the French vernacular Passions, from the *Passion du Palatinus* to the *Passion d'Arras*, from the *Passion Semur* to the *Passion d'Autun*. In the German vernacular dramatic tradition the role of the Virgin was generally even more developed than in the French or vernacular Passion plays. In such German Passion plays as the Tyrol *Passion*, the St. Gall *Passion*, the Frankfurt *Passion*, the Alsfeld *Passion*, the Virgin occupies the center of the stage throughout the scene on Mount Calvary. In Italy, in the vernacular Passions and particularly in the *Laude*, the Virgin achieves prominence by playing a significant dramatic role in the culminating moments of the divine tragedy.

This later lingering over Mary's suffering was due primarily to the influence of the *Meditations Vitae Christi*, now assigned to the early fourteenth century and ascribed to the Franciscan monk Joannes de Caulibus. The whole of the *Meditationes*, which were written by a cleric for a spiritual daughter, although based on the Gospels and the Acts of the Apostles, avoids the parables and the prodigies contained in them. The *Meditationes* enlarge the bare outlines of canonical narrative, invent and invest new scenes of the Passion with lively color and concrete detail, elaborate the anguish of Mary, enlarge the hyperdulia of the "mater dolorosa," pass over dogma in order to represent a personal and poignant human experience for the pious to contemplate. Whereas the Gospels appealed to the intelligence, the *Meditationes* appeal to the heart. And it is the pathos and human detail of the *Meditationes* which fill the Passion plays, art and literature of the later Middle Ages. The earliest extant Latin Passion plays are more concerned with the sacrifice on the Cross.

To conclude, then, the separation of the *Planctus Mariae* from the Passion proper and the fact that numerous *Planctus* have come down to us, have, in general, contributed to the idea that the Passion Play may have derived from the *Planctus*. Since, however, no extant *Planctus* precedes the highly developed Passion play of Montecassino, and since this Passion includes only a rudimentary *Planctus* of three lines it seems clear that the *Planctus* is not the germ or stimulus of this Passion play, nor probably of others in the twelfth and thirteenth centuries, but a lyrical piece which could intensify the Crucifixion scene or simply co-exist with the Passion as a separate type of lyric.

NOTES

1. Karl Young, *The Drama of the Medieval Church*, 2 vols. (Oxford, 1933), 1, 12.
2. D.M. Inguanez, "Un dramma della Passione del Secolo XII," *Miscellanea Cassinese* 12 (1936), 7-38; reprinted, with the addition of a Sulmona fragment in *Miscellanea Cassinese* 17 (1939), 7-50.
3. Young, 1, 492.
4. Benjamin Hunningher, *The Origin of the Theater* (Amsterdam, 1955), p. 68.
5. Grace Frank, *The Medieval French Drama* (Oxford, 1954), p. 29; Hardin Craig, *English Religious Drama* (Oxford, 1955), pp. 42-43, 255; Hans Heinrich Borcherdt, "Geschichte des deutschen Theaters" in Wolfgang Stammler's *Deutsche Philologie im Aufriss*, vol. 3 (Berlin, 1957), 418-558, cols. 428-89; W.L.

Smoldon, "Liturgical Drama" in Anselm Hughes' *Early Medieval Music to 1300* [New Oxford History of Music, II] (London, 1954), p. 194.

6. Wilfred Werner, *Studien zu den Passions—und Osterspielen* (Berlin, 1963), pp. 19–20; also O.B. Hardison Jr., *Christian Rite and Christian Drama in the Middle Ages* (Baltimore, 1965), p. 225.

7. Young, 1, 492.

8. Ibid., Erwin Wolff, "Die Terminologie des mittelalterlichen Dramas in bedeutungsgeschichtlicher Sicht," *Anglia* 78 (1960), 7–8.

9. Joseph A. Jungmann, *The Mass of the Roman Rite: Its Origins and Development*, 2 vols. (New York, Boston, 1950), 1, 177.

10. Migne, *P.L.*, 105 vol. 989. "The sacraments ought to have some kind of similarity to those events of life for which they are sacraments. For this reason, the priest should be like Christ, just as the bread and the wine are like the body of Christ. Thus, the sacrifice of the priest at the altar is, so to speak, like the sacrifice of Christ on the Cross."

11. Ibid., 172, col. 570. "It should be realized that those who recited tragic dramas in the theater used to portray to the people in their gestures the actions of heroes. In the same manner, our tragic actor portrays by his gestures to the Christian people the heroic struggle of Christ in the theater of the church and he impresses on them the victory of his own redemption."

12. Marie-Thérèse d'Alverny, ed., *Alain de Lille. Textes Inédits* (Paris, 1965), p. 280.

13. Solange Corbin, in *La déposition liturgique du Christ au Vendredi Saint* (Paris, 1960), clearly indicates, pp. 202–4, that the Passion Plays do not derive from the *Depositio*.

14. Karl Young, "Observations on the Origin of the medieval Passion Play," *PMLA* 25 (1910), 309–54; also his *Drama of the Medieval Church*, op. cit., 1, p. 539.

15. Paolo Ferretti, "Il canto della Passione nella Settimana Santa," *Rivista Liturgica* 5 (1918), 70; Vincenzo Coosemans, "Il canto del *Passio*," *Rivista Liturgica* 6 (1919), 54–5; G. Römer, "Die Liturgie des Karfreitags," *Zeitschrift für Katolische Theologie* 77 (1955), 64.

16. R.W. Southern, *The Making of the Middle Ages* (New Haven, 1959), p. 232; Dom Jean Leclercq, *L'amour des lettres et le désir de Dieu* (Paris, 1957), p. 240.

17. Migne, *P.L.*, 183. St. Bernard, *Sermones in Cantica*, Sermo 43, 4, col 995.

18. P. Pourrat, *La spiritualité chrétienne*, 2 vols. (Paris, 1947-51), 2, 481; Félix Vernet, *La spiritualité médiévale* (Paris, 1929), p. 18.

19. Gabriel Millet, *L'iconographie de l'Evangile* (Paris, 1916), p. 398; Paul Thoby, *Le crucifix des origines au Concile de Trente* (Nantes, 1959), p. 79; H.L. Grondijs, *L'iconographie byzantine du Crucifié mort sur la Croix* (Utrecht, 1947), p. 4; Bernard Teyssèdre, *Le sacramentaire de Gellone* (Paris, 1959), p. 110.

20. J.R. Martin, "The Dead Christ on the Cross in Byzantine Art," *Late Classical and Mediaeval Studies in Honor of Albert Mathias Friend Jr.* (Princeton, 1955), p. 189; Victor Leroquais, *Les sacramentaires et les missels manuscrits des*

Bibliothèques Publiques de France, 3 vols. (Paris, 1924), 1, p. xxxv; M. Didron, *Iconographie chrétienne* (Paris, 1843), p. 235; Grondijs, op. cit., p. 25.

21. Martin loc. cit., p. 192.

22. Emile Bertaux, *L'art dans l'Italie méridionale* (Paris, 1904), pp. 201–2; Dom Agostino Maria Latil, *Le miniature nei Rotoli dell' Exultet* (Montecassino, 1899); Paolo d'Ancona, *La miniature italienne du Xe au XVIe siècle* (Paris, 1925), p. 4; David Diringer, *The Illuminated Book: Its History and Production* (London, 1958), p. 295.

23. Dom Teodoro Leuterman, Ordo Casinensis Hebdomadae Maioris, *Miscellanea Cassinese* 20 (1941), 82.

24. P.F. Russo, "Attività artistico-culturale del Monachismo calabro-greco anteriormente all'epoca normanna," *Atti dell'VIII Congresso di Studi Bizantini* 1 (Rom, 1953), 463–75.

25. Paul Weber, *Geistliches Schauspiel und kirchliche Kunst* (Stuttgart, 1894), p. 52.

26. Eduard Wechssler, *Die Romanischen Marienklagen* (Halle, 1893), p. 98.

27. George C. Taylor, "The English Planctus Mariae," *MP* 4 (1906-07), 633.

28. Young, 1, p. 538.

29. Ibid., 495–98.

30. W. Lipphardt, "Marienklagen und Liturgie," *Jahrbuch für Liturgiewissenschaft* 12 (1932), 201–4; also his "Studien zu den Marienklagen und Germanische Totenklagen," *Beiträge zur Geschichte der Deutschen Sprache und Literatur* 58 (1934); 394–96.

31. Richard Kienast, "Die deutschsprachige Lyrik des Mittelalters" in Wolfgang Stammler's *Deutsche Philologie im Aufriss*, 2 (Berlin, 1954), p. 890.

32. Giovanni Cremaschi, "*Planctus Mariae:* Nuovi Testi Inediti," *Aevum* 29 (1955), 394; G. Vecchi, "Innodia e dramma sacro," *Studi Mediolatini e Volgari*, 1 (1953): 225–37.

33. Young, 1, pp. 507–12; Vincenzo de Bartholomaeis, *Origini della poesia drammatica Italiana* (Torino, 1952), pp. 482–85.

34. Young, 1, pp. 498–99.

35. Cremaschi, loc. cit., 393–468.

36. For the text of the "Qui per viam pergitis," see Young, 1, pp. 500-502.

37. Giuseppe Billanovich, "Uffizi drammatici della Chiesa Padovana" *Rivista Italiana del Dramma* 4 (Gennaio, 1940), 72–100. The *planctus* found by Billanovich is the very text referred to by Dondi and which Karl Young unsuccessfully tried to locate (see Young, 1, p. 700).

38. Wilhelm Creizenach, *Geschichte des Neuren Dramas*, 5 vols. (Halle, 2nd ed., 1911), 1, p. 248; Theo Meier, *Die Gestalt Marias im geistlichen Schauspiel des deutschen Mittelalters* (Berlin, 1959), pp. 178–79.

39. Maria Sofia de Vito, *L'origine del dramma liturgico* (Milan, 1938), p. 164.

40. Craig, op. cit., p. 47; Grace Frank, too, in *The Medieval French Drama*,

p. 29, feels that, although "potentially dramatic," the *Planctus* "remained lyric and static."

41. Hardin Craig, "The Origin of the Passion Play: Matters of Theory as Well as Fact," *University of Missouri Studies* 20 (1946–47), 83–90.

42. Inguanez (1939 ed.), pp. 41–42.

43. Young, 1, p. 538.

44. Emile Mâle, *Religious Art in France in the XII Century* (New York, 1913), p. 122.

45. Preface to the Easter Sunday Mass.

46. Migne, *P.L.*, 182, cols. 1133–42.

47. Ibid., 159, cols. 271–90.

48. For text see F.J.E. Raby, *Christian Latin Poetry* (Oxford, 1953), p. 440.

49. A.C. Peltier, ed., *S. Bonaventurae Meditationes Vitae Christi*, in *Opera Omnia*, 12 (Paris, 1968).

50. Migne, *P.L.*, 182, col. 1135. "My loving son turned his benign face towards me, his weeping mother, and with tender words wished to console me. But no comfort could I derive and weeping replied: O son, how gladly would I die for you. If the son must die, so let the mother also be crucified. My only son, my sweet progeny, do not leave me here destitute, but allow that I die with you."

51. Ibid., 184 , cols. 742–67; 770–72; 954–66.

52. Ibid., cols. 1319–24.

53. *S. Bonaventurae Opera Omnia*, 10 Vols. (Quaracchi, 1898), 8, p. 120. "Since man's devotional fervor is nourished by means of a frequent recollection of Christ's passion, it is necessary, therefore, that he who wishes to keep unextinguished this devotion should always contemplate with the eyes of the soul Christ suffering and dying on the Cross."

54. Raby, op. cit., p. 418. The motto seems to be derived from St. Paul (Ad Galatas 6, 14, '*Mihi autem absit gloriari, nisi in cruce Domini Iesu Christi*').

55. A most extended and learned analysis of St. Francis' Passion piety is found in P. Oktavian von Rieden, "Das Leiden Christi im Leben des Hl. Franziskus von Assisi: Eine Quellenvergleichende Untersuchung im Lichte der zeitgenösischen Passionsfrömmigkeit," *Collectanea Franciscana*, 18–19 (1948–49), 45–142.

56. Raby, op. cit., p. 423; Arnaldo Fortini, *La lauda in Assisi e le origini del teatro italiano* (Assisi, 1961), p. 382, ; Amédée P. de Zedelgem, "Aperçu historique sur la dévotion au chemin de la Croix," *Collectanea Franciscana* 18–19 (1948–49), 45–142.

57. Blume and Dreves, *Analecta Hymnica Medii Aevi* (New York and London, 1961), 50, pp. 571–73.

58. *De Obitu Valentiniani*. Cap. XXXIX, *P.L.*, 16, col. 1431; also in *Expositio Evangelii Secundum Lucam*, *P.L.*, 15, cols. 1930–31.

59. P. Gabriel M. Roschini, "De modo quo B. Virgo animi dolorem sustinuit," in his *Mariologia* (Rome, 1948), 2, p. 210.

60. Lipphardt, "Studien zu den Marienklagen...", loc. cit., 395.

61. A. Mingana, "The Lament of the Virgin and the Martyrdom of Pilate" *Woodbrooke Studies* 2 (Manchester, 1928), 411–530; also E. Cothenet, "Marie dans les Apocryphes," *Maria* 6 (Paris, 1961), 111–12. One of the earliest examples of the *Staurotheotokia*, in the Eastern Church, is the one composed by Romanos in the fifth century. (See Joannes Baptista Pitra, *Analecta Sacra* 1 [Paris, 1876], pp. 101–7.) Jacob of Sarug (c. 451–521), the well-known sixth century Syrian poet, in a poem entitled "De Transitu," offers an already fairly developed conception of Mary as the *Mater Dolorosa*; and Simeon Metaphrastes, living in the tenth century, wrote a *Lament of the Blessed Virgin* which anticipates the medieval *planctus Mariae*.

62. Migne, *P.G.*, 6, *Dialogus cum Tryphone Judaeo, Caput*. 100, cols. 710–11.

63. Ibid., 7, *Contra Haereses, Lib. III, Caput. XXII*, cols. 958–60.

64. *P.L.*, 2, *De Carne Christi, Caput. VII*, cols. 781–82.

65. Ibid., 16, *Epistola LXIII, Caput, 33*, col. 1249.

66. Ibid., 22, *Epistola XXII*, col. 408.

67. Sister Mary Vincentine Gripkey, *The Blessed Virgin as Mediatrix in the Latin and Old French Legend prior to the Fourteenth Century* (Washington, 1938), p. 11.

68. Henri Barré, *Prières anciennes de l'Occident à la Mère du Sauveur* (Paris, 1963), p. 125.

69. Dom F. Leclercq, "Dévotion et théologie mariales dans le Monachisme Bénédictin," *Maria*, 2 (Paris, 1952), 567.

70. Hilda Graef, *Mary: a History of Doctrine and Devotion*, 2 vols. (New York, 1963–65), 2, 215.

71. Ibid., p. 239.

72. William F. Hogan, *Christ's Redemptive Sacrifice* (Englewood Cliffs, 1965), p. 101.

73. *P.L.*, 189 cols. 1726–27.

74. H.P.J.M. Ahsmann, *Le culte de la sainte Vierge et la littérature française du moyen âge* (Utrecht, 1930), pp. 10–30.

75. M.M. Davy, "La présence de la Vierge au XIIe siècle," *La Table Ronde* 129 (September, 1958), 106; also Walter Delius, *Geschichte der Marienverehrung* (Munich, Basel, 1963), pp. 159–66.

76. Emile Mâle, *L'Art religieux de la fin du moyen âge* (Paris, 1946), p. 122.

77. Angelus Luis, "Evolutio historica doctrinae de Compassione B. Mariae Virginis," *Marianum* 5 (1943), 274–76; Lutz Machensen, "Mitterlalterliche Tragödien: Gedanken uber Wesen und Grenzen des Mittelalters," *Festschrift für Wolfgang Stammler* (Berlin, 1953): 99.

78. Ibid., p. 276; Wilmart, *Auteurs spirituels*, op. cit., pp. 505–9.

79. *In Nativitatem B.M.*, I, in *P.L.*, CXLIV, col. 748 A.

80. *P.L.*, 159, cols. 271–90.

81. Ibid., 158 cols. 902–5.

82. Ibid., 182, cols. 1133–42.

83. Jean Leclercq, "Jean de Fécamp et S. Bernard dans les florilèges anciens,"

Analecta Monastica 20 (1948), p. 103.

84. Barré, *Prières anciennes*, op. cit., p. 229.

85. *P.L.*, 189, col. 1727.

86. Ibid., 159, col. 567.

87. Ibid., 196, col. 483.

88. Ibid., 183, cols. 437–38.

89. Henri Barré, "Le 'Planctus Mariae' attribué à Saint Bernard," *Revue d'Ascétique et de Mystique* 28 (1952), 245–46.

90. Stephen Beissel, *Geschichte der Verehrung Marias in Deutschland* (Freiburg, 1909), pp. 379 ff.; Corbin, *La Deposition*, op. cit., pp. 210–13.

91. Mario Apollonio, *Storia del teatro italiano*, 2 vols. (Firenze, 1943), 1, 190.

92. A fourteenth-century Statute of Gubbio's (Italy) Company of the Crucifix states, for instance, that on Good Friday evening, should the prior so desire, the Confraternity brothers shall gather in some church "*in qua ecclesia lacrimosas laudes et cantus dolorosos et amara Lamenta Virginis Matris vidue proprio orbate Filio cum reverentia populo representent, magis ad lacrimas attendentes quam ad verba.*" (In G. Mazzatinti, "I disciplinati di Gubbio e i loro Uffizi drammatici," *Giornale di Filologia Romanza* 3 [1880]: 96.)

93. Theodor Wolpers, "Englische Marienlyrik im Mittelalter," *Anglia*, 69 (1950), 21.

EVERYMAN AND THE PARABLE
OF THE TALENTS

V. A. Kolve

MANY SCHOLARS at work over several decades have done much to discover the sources of *Everyman*. We have learned that it owes something to the traditions of the Dance of Death, to confessional manuals, to treatises on the art of holy dying, to a medieval schema that divides all human endowments into gifts of Nature, Fortune and Grace; and most important of all, we have been shown its likeness to a testing-of-friends story (Buddhist in origin) that appears first shaped to a Christian moral in the Greek *Barlaam and Ioasaph* of the eleventh century. Professor A.C. Cawley, in his recent edition of the play, has summarized and significantly extended those enquiries.[1] Though I shall propose in this paper a new and more inclusive way of describing the play's central concerns, I have no wish to forsake any of this genealogy of relationship already established. The literary kindred of the play called *Everyman* are as numerous as the centrality of its subject would suggest. That subject is nothing less than man's dying and doom.

But there remains a number of things unexplained and unaccounted for. Scholarship has passed over in silence some facts that bulk very large. Consider, for example, the way the title-page names the central action:

Here begynneth a treatyse how the hye Fader of heuen sendeth Dethe to somon euery creature to come and gyue a-counte of theyr lyues in this worlde / and is in maner of a morall playe.

Notice that the play is *not* entitled "A treatyse how a man shulde lerne dye," or "...how a man his trewe frendes may knowe," or "...what be yiftes of Kynde, Fortune, and Grace," though such formulas are what a careful reading of the scholarship surrounding the play might lead one to expect. The audience will of course learn something about all three subjects—as titles, none would be wholly misleading—but they were not what the printer and/or dramatist thought the play was about: that they defined instead as a summons to ready and render accounts.

The playing-text indeed makes necessary that description. The words "reckoning" and "account" occur (in varying grammatical forms) more than twenty-five times in the play, often together, and always at moments of high urgency, where most meaning is being gathered in fewest words.[2] I propose to give them some close attention, and wish to begin with two summary foreclosures. First of all, we must not ascribe this language to the dramatist's unique invention, to the particular poetry of his play; as will be seen, it is language very common in relation to the Doom.[3] And more important, we must not confuse this summons to an accounting with the sublime image of Revelations 20:12, 15:

And I saw the dead, great and small, standing in the presence of the throne. And the books were opened; and another book was opened, which was the book of life. And the dead were judged by those things which were written in the books, according to their works.... And whosoever was not found written in the book of life was cast into the pool of fire. [Douay translation]

We must not confuse these images, though I suspect many have. These books are kept in heaven, they are part of a mystery. Everyman, in strong contrast, must bring with him his own account-book—it is a literal stage-property—and his urgent task is to ready and "clere" it. His greatest concern is (in terms of sources) nothing indebted to the high mystery of Apocalypse, but is instead a thing smaller, humbler, more precise.[4] God orders Everyman to *"bring with hym* a sure rekenynge"(70).

The search for a possible source for this action will be made easier if we note how closely it is related to another recurring theme of the play: the notion that life and goods are "lent," not given. Everyman is forced to confront that sad truth at several crucial moments of loss,[5] in exchanges like the following:

> Dethe. What, wenest thou thy lyue is gyuen the,
>   And thy worldely gooddes also?
> Everyman. I had wende so, veryle.
> Dethe. Nay, nay, it was but lende the.... (161-164)

Later, as his understanding grows, Everyman will recount his duty in that same way:

> Of all my workes I must shewe
> How I haue lyued and my dayes spent;
> Also of yll dedes that I haue vsed
> In my tyme, syth lyfe was me lent.... (338-344)

Words like "reckoning," "account-making," "lending," and "spending," compose the essential verbal matrix of the play; and the account-book Everyman brings with him is the emblem of their interrelationship. It is what the play most urgently concerns.

A fifteenth-century English poet in the act of contemplating the nearness of his own death offers evidence that such an association of ideas is not novel, and can furnish a clue to its ultimate source. John Lydgate, in his *Testament*, writes:

> Age is crope In, calleth me to my grave,
> To make rekenyng how I my tyme haue spent,
> Baryne of vertu, allas, who shall me saue,
> Fro fendes daunger tacounte for my talent,
> But Iesu be my staf and my potent,
> Ouerstreite audite is like tencombre me,
> Or dome be youen, but mercy be present
> To all that knele to Iesu on ther kne.[6]

The only important word in this verse not found in *Everyman*, other than those suggesting an advanced old age, is the word "talent." But where that word occurs, these others occur also. And where these others occur but the word "talent" is missing, it is, I shall argue, the necessary explanation of them. The parable which gives meaning to Lydgate's verse furnishes for *Everyman* also an intellectual structure just below the surface of the play, and from it many of the play's characters, the most distinctive part of its language, and the logic of its total action derive. It is less a new "source" for *Everyman*, than the source behind the sources: the covered logic of an action that made that action coherent and inevitable. Interrelationships between medieval texts are sometimes so complex that it is possible to name those nearest and most like without having looked at the most important of all.

Because it will be our steady concern in what follows, I wish to set out here the parable of the talents, entire, as it is found in Matthew 25:14-30:

For even as a man going into a far country called his servants and delivered to them his goods;

And to one he gave five talents, and to another two, and to another one, to everyone according to his proper ability; and immediately he took his journey.

And he that had received the five talents went his way and traded with the same and gained other five.

And in like manner he that had received the two gained other two.

But he that had received the one, going his way, digged into the earth and hid his lord's money.

But after a long time the lord of those servants came and reckoned with them.

And he that had received the five talents, coming, brought other five talents, saying: Lord, thou didst deliver to me five talents. Behold, I have gained other five over and above.

His lord said to him: Well done, good and faithful servant; because thou hast been faithful over a few things, I will place thee over many things. Enter thou into the joy of thy lord.

And he also that had received the two talents came and said: Lord, thou deliveredst two talents to me. Behold, I have gained other two.

His lord said to him: Well done, good and faithful servant; because thou hast been faithful over a few things, I will place thee over many things. Enter thou into the joy of thy lord.

But he that had received the one talent came and said: Lord, I know that thou art a hard man; thou reapest where thou hast not sown and gatherest where thou has not strewed.

And, being afraid, I went and hid thy talent in the earth. Behold, here thou hast that which is thine.

And his lord answering said to him: Wicked and slothful servant, thou knewest that I reap where I sow not and gather where I have not strewed.

Thou oughtest therefore to have committed my money to the bankers; and at my coming I should have received my own with usury.

Take ye away therefore the talent from him and give it him that hath ten talents.

For to everyone that hath shall be given, and he shall abound: but, from him that hath not, that also which he seemeth to have shall be taken away.

And the unprofitable servant cast ye out into the exterior darkness. There shall be weeping and gnashing of teeth.

Any modern commentator will tell you that a talent was originally a unit of weight which became also a unit of monetary value, its precise worth depending on the metal it measured. But that clarifies only the literal sense of the parable. The talents are obviously used here as a figure of speech, as a way of talking about something else. Indeed, it is only because Christ used them to talk about something else that the word "talent" is current still. Its present signification descends from the glosses of the Fathers concerning Christ's real subject, and therefore stands now for natural endowment, ability, capacity. It does so in French, Italian, Spanish, and English.

Though this text from Matthew will be our chief concern, it is not possible to separate it entirely from two other parables which also concern talents loaned or placed in trust—not possible, because medieval writers and preachers did not always distinguish between them. One is the version offered by Luke 19: 12-27, differing in some details but clearly an alternate account of the same teaching. The other is found in Matthew 18, beginning at the twenty-third verse:

Therefore is the kingdom of heaven likened to a king who would take an account of his servants.

And, when he had begun to take the account, one was brought to him that owed him ten thousand talents.

> And, as he had not wherewith to pay it, his lord commanded that he should be sold, and his wife and children and all that he had, and payment to be made.
>
> But that servant falling down besought him, saying: Have patience with me and I will pay thee all.

The king has pity and releases him from his debt. The servant later chances to meet a man who owes him a hundred pence in turn. He demands an immediate settlement, and when the other pleads his inability to pay, the king's servant has him thrown into prison. The king, hearing of this, summons his servant again, charges him with his failure to forgive as he himself had been forgiven, and delivers him to torturers until the debt be paid.

This parable is entirely separate from the other two, but I mention it now because it also bears an important relationship to *Everyman*, and because the word "talent" links all three parables in ways medieval authors were not always concerned to keep separate. The parable from Matthew 25, however, is much the most important—for its narrative power, its richer detail, the greater significance of its surrounding matter (the wise and foolish virgins precede it, the corporal deeds of mercy follow), and perhaps as a result of all the above, the greater patristic attention paid it over the course of several centuries. It would be worth our present attention if only to explain the play's central figure, a man summoned to render account of goods lent him for a time and now recalled. But in fact its importance for *Everyman* is far more extensive, in ways patristic commentary on the parable alone can make clear. I wish to suggest some of those ways, one instance at a time.

Let me begin with the desertions—that movement-into-aloneness generic to tragedy which is here represented by the betrayals of Felawship, Kynrede, and Goodes, and later by the departure of Beaute, Strength, Dyscrecion, and V. Wyttes. The tale of the man who has three friends, two of whom betray him in his greatest need (a tale existing in numerous versions and many languages, deriving ultimately from *Barlaam and Ioasaph*) has long been recognized as a source of this action. Everyman does test his friends and some of them bear names deriving from prose moralizations of that story. The first friend is most frequently explained as standing for Riches, or the World; the second as figuring Wife and Kindred (sometimes including Friends); and the third friend, too little loved but alone faithful, is named Good Deeds, or Charity, or Christ. The relationship is close and vital. But on its own it is not enough. These analogues offer no help in accounting for the second set of desertions, the second tragic movement of the play. For those, we are accustomed to refer to the *ars moriendi*, which does indeed concern the experience of death, but in ways a good deal less physical and interior than the play's second part.[7] The *ars*, it is true, does speak of wife and children and riches as temptations to a dying man, for he is likely to turn to them for help, uselessly, and in ways ultimately dangerous to his soul. But, in terms of literary genetics, that is merely to account again for some features already provided by the three-friends story. The subject of the *ars moriendi* is emphatically *not* the physical process of dying: it insists that in the moment of extremity only spiritual matters are worth attention. In short, these two sources between them can account for Felawship, Kynrede, Cosyn, Goodes, Good Dedes. A great deal, but not all. The parable of the talents and patristic commentary upon it, in strong contrast, can furnish us not only with the central figure of a man summoned to a reckoning, and with the characters just named, but also with those characters excluded so far: Beaute, Strength, Dyscrecion, V. Wyttes, Knowledge, and even Confessyon. It does so in two different ways.

The first way, and the more generally inclusive, is developed by those commentaries that work from the idea of talents *per se*, ignoring (as does the gospel of Luke) the 5–2–1 numerology of Matthew. This tradition goes back at least as far as St. John Chrysostom in the fourth century,[8] but I shall quote from the vastly more influential statement of it made by Gregory the Great at the end of his brilliant homily on the parable—a version incorporated by Rabanus Maurus into his own eight-book commentary on Matthew written some two centuries later.[9] Gregory writes:

There is no one who can truly say: I have received no talent at all, there is nothing about which I can be required to give a reckoning. For even the very smallest of gifts will be charged as a talent to the account of every poor man. For one man has received understanding [*intelligentia*] and owes the ministry of preaching by reason of that talent. Another has received earthly goods, and owes alms-giving from his talent, out of his property. Another has received neither understanding of inner things [*internorum intelligentia*] nor wealth of worldly goods [*rerum affluentia*], but he has learned an art or skill by which he lives, and this very skill is charged to his account as the receiving of a talent. Another has acquired none of these things, but nevertheless has perhaps come to be on terms of friendship [*familiaritas*] with a rich man; he has therefore received the talent of friendship. So if he does not speak to him on behalf of the poor, he is condemned for not using his talent.[10]

Already this could suggest to a dramatist the characters Knowledge, Goodes, and Felawship. And in his insistence that the very smallest of gifts—those common even to the poor—must be recognized as talents and put out to use, Gregory may be taken to imply that humbler inventory that Chrysostom had named earlier:

For the talents here are each person's ability, whether in the way of protection, or in money, or in teaching, or in what thing soever of the kind. . . . For this end God gave us speech, and hands, and feet, and strength of body, and mind, and understanding. . . .[11]

Here Strength makes a separate appearance, and Dyscrecion (mind) as well, to single out only those not already named in the passage from Gregory. A commentary long attributed to the Venerable Bede, but actually based on Rabanus, concludes its exposition of the parable by emphasizing this same kind of open-ended applicability, as I suppose any of us would if we were asked (without preparation) to suggest its general meaning: "These things may be interpreted in many ways as concerning charity, ability and knowledge." The *Glossa ordinaria* instructs in a similar mode: "Note that what is given to each one in worldly or spiritual things is charged to his account, as the talent for which he will have to give a reckoning when the Lord returns."[12]

But patristic tradition can offer further and more particular help, for the numbers in Matthew also invited theological speculation. A 5–2–1 progression, with its multiples, necessarily exercised the imagination of a culture that thought numbers one of the hidden languages of God. Because no number in Scripture could be without spiritual meaning, however enigmatic, several explanations were made over the course of centuries. The earliest known to me, that of St. Hilary of Poitiers from the mid-fourth century, is especially concerned with how the Gentiles won the inheritance promised the Jews. The servant who received five talents is read as a figure for those people of the law who received the five books of Moses and who doubled that trust by the faith of the Gospel, recognizing the sacraments as having been foreshadowed in the law. Because those persons thereby fulfill the commandments in a new way, they are justified by both law and faith. These are, I take it, the Jews who accept Christ, of whom the apostles themselves stand as first exemplars.

Hilary interprets the servant who received two talents as standing for those people of the Gentiles who have faith in their heart and confess by their mouth that Christ is Lord—a capacity for inner faith and public witness are the two talents, which they double by good works, authenticating their faith through action. It is with reference to them that the unprofitable servant charges his master with reaping where he has not sown, for the final harvest is here foreseen to be mostly of the Gentiles, instead of the seed of Abraham to whom the Messiah was promised. The first servant offers works doubled by faith; the second servant, faith doubled by deeds.

And the third servant, it follows, must typify the Jews still living in darkness, rejecting Christ and His gospel, carnal in their understanding, thinking to be justified by the law alone. The teaching of Christ they hid in the earth, neither using it themselves nor wishing others to use it. And their fate will be terrible: "For to them that have the use of the Gospels, even the honor of the law is given; but from him that has not the faith of Christ, even the honor which he seems to have of the law will be taken away."[13]

This early version of the parable's meaning is without consequence for *Everyman*, as is part of another tradition, rather closely allied, summarized by Rabanus Maurus so: "The first servant, in being given five talents, received the five books of the law, which,

77

by the doctrine and fulfillment of the ten commandments, he increased. The second, in being given the two talents, received the two Testaments, and these, in a moral and mystical sense, he doubled by piously spreading their teaching abroad. The third, in the likeness of one talent, received the gift of grace, but he hid it in earthly pleasures, and was therefore cast into hell, for he produced no profit from it.''[14] Such a reading of the two talents is not uncommon, and the interpretation of the single talent as grace buried in earthly pleasures has some obvious bearing on *Everyman*. But a tradition descending from St. Jerome is another matter altogether, more useful to preachers concerned with the moral lives of their parishioners, more widely disseminated and influential, and more steadily illuminating for our play. In his longer commentary on Matthew, Jerome explains that the five talents are to be understood as the five senses—sight, hearing, taste, smell, touch— which are exactly equivalent to the character V. Wyttes in *Everyman;* that the two talents are to be understood as *intelligentia et opera*, which almost as certainly furnish us the characters Knowledge and Good Dedes (his context suggests an affirmative, not neutral, meaning for both terms) ; and that the one talent is to be understood as *ratio* alone, which I take to be synonymous with the character Dyscrecion. This version of the numbers was transmitted by Isidore of Seville in his *Allegoriae quaedam sacrae scripturae* and thence by Rabanus Maurus in his *De universo*.[15]

One of the identifications I have just made demands fuller and more careful statement, for it addresses one of the most difficult questions in *Everyman* scholarship. Namely: is the character Knowledge to be understood in something like our modern sense of that term [*scientia, intelligentia*]? Or does it stand instead for the even-then rarer, and now archaic, medieval sense of "acknowledge," naming that part of the sacrament of penance which concerns a full confession of sins? The latter sense was first proposed in 1947 by H. de Vocht, and has since been skillfully supported by several others. It is an attractive idea, and I was once persuaded by it; but close attention to the morphology of the word in our text—it occurs only as a noun, never as a verb—and, more to the present point, evidence from patristic commentary on the parable of the talents, both suggest the older and simpler answer is probably correct.[16] Good Dedes and Knowledge are linked in the play as intimately as are *opera* and *intelligentia* in explanations of the two talents given the second servant. Indeed, the tradition just named, that of Jerome, Isidore, and Rabanus, can help a good deal in clarifying the relationship of certain allegorical characters in the play to others closely allied. The gift of the five senses [V. Wyttes] is defined by them as a knowledge of external things, that is, the receiving of sense data. Reason [Dyscrecion] separates us from the beasts, and comprises the ability to interpret such data. And Knowedge in its turn is the product of reason working perfectly upon sense data : reason not blinded by earthly concerns, not stupidly tenacious of the literal, but seeking instead the spiritual truth that lies hidden within all phenomena.[17] In *Everyman* it is clear, I think, that Knowledge exemplifies this deepest kind of understanding. As a character, she has knowledge of Confession and its efficacy, and is a useful guide to it; but she speaks many other truths as well.

The parable of the talents, then, can explain the figure of Everyman as a man summoned to render accounts; and, better than the more immediately proximate sources, it offers a comprehensive rationale for the other *dramatis personae*, both interior and exterior, whom he confronts in the course of this action. It also offers help in what must be always one of the crucial tasks of criticism: the attempt to define with maximum precision what *happens* within a work of art.

For instance, there is another group of words closely associated in the play, and nearly as insistently central as those concerned with "accounts" and "reckoning." More than twenty-five times, the words "pylgrymage," "vyage," or "iourney" occur, and these, too, despite their linguistic weight, have never had any close attention.[18] Perhaps this is because the idea of pilgrimage as a figure for all human life was so common in the Middle Ages; even now it seems to require no glossing. Besides, Everyman goes a journey before our eyes, from one friend to another and finally into the grave.

But again, as with Everyman's account book, if that *is* the explanation of the scholarly silence, then I think that we have mistaken the matter, conflating two metaphors allied but separate, only one of which is really at the center of the play. The pilgrimage in question is not that "of human life"—in the manner of *The Canterbury Tales* or *The Castle of Perseverance* or Deguilleville's *Le Pèlerinage de la Vie Humaine*. That pilgrimage has been underway since Everyman's birth and is hardly spoken of here. It does not add up to news, or require a message of command. The errand assigned to Dethe:

> Go thou to Eueryman
> And shewe hym, in my name,
> A pylgrymage he must on hym take (66-68)

employs a different metaphor, and concerns a new contingency in a life already at the full. In the pilgrimage of life, Everyman's friends have been his constant companions, but in this new and "longe" journey, their constancy is at an end. The latter is, quite simply, the death-journey of the soul to Judgment—Deguilleville's *Le Pèlerinage de l'Ame*—and most of the play is devoted to showing the soul freeing itself from earth so it can depart. That brief and final action—a swift and simple journey upwards—alone is the pilgrimage suddenly ordained and so inadequately prepared for. The angel describes it so:

> Come, excellente electe spouse, to Iesu!
> Here aboue thou shalte go
>
> . . . .
>
> Now shalte thou in to the heuenly spere,
> Vnto the which all ye shall come
> That lyueth well before the daye of dome. (894-901)

That journey was first made by Christ in His ascension, and to it the parable of the talents was always understood to refer in its opening words: *Sicut enim homo peregre proficiscens*...(Matthew) or *Homo quidam nobilis abiit in regionem longinquam*... (Luke), Englished by the Wycliffite Bible, "Sothely as a man goynge fer in pilgrimage," and "Sum noble man wente in to a fer cuntree ...."[19] According to the Fathers, Christ used the terms *peregre* and *in regionem longinquam* because he was foretelling His ascension in the flesh. The mystery of the Incarnation, in which God united Himself with man's kind forever, made His long journey also a pilgrimage, for that word, in the Bible as well as in countless medieval texts, has about it always the suggestion of exile, of finding oneself in a country foreign and potentially hostile. The soul's true home is heaven, but the flesh will go there a stranger and afraid.

I would not wish to claim, in the absence of these other relationships, that *Everyman's* use of pilgrimage as a metaphor for the soul-journey need be explained by reference to the parable of the talents. It was available in many other places. But the fact is that the parable, which is *necessary* on other grounds, does make those words available, uses them as a part of its vital meaning, and may therefore help account for their great frequency and importance in the play: the pilgrimage of Everyman's soul recapitulates the first of Christ's journeys in the parable. What can easily seem to us the "longe journey"—all those desperate wanderings in the *platea*, the search for companionship into the grave—is really born of the allegorical mode itself, that same formal and artistic necessity that also fragments a man's personality and experience of life into two sets of "friends." Its purpose is merely to disentangle, to make consecutive, spatial, and linear, the extremely complex process of how a man dies. Each stage of human dying—that mysterious transition from being to apparent non-being—is rendered as a separate event, but its real-life referent may of course be much shorter or much longer. The duration of the play need represent barely more than the moment of death itself, when light and life fade altogether, though it must be long enough for a motion of contrition within the soul and for the receiving of sacraments on one's death-bed. The, desertions—friends, kin, goods, beauty, strength, the five senses— are in some sense simultaneous, for none of these is utterly and irretrievably lost until they are lost altogether, at the moment of extinction. To separate them is simply to make the totality of that loss more readily apprehensible by the mind and the imagination. But the Everyman specific to this play is possibly youthful and certainly no more than in his prime ("O Dethe, thou comest whan I had thee leest in mynde"), and this division-into-parts, native to allegory, is also meant to image another kind of dying: that which comes to the old, who do lose these things slowly, remorselessly. The frenzied movement here-and-there that we see in the *platea* is ultimately that of the soul of *any* man, whatever his age, as it struggles to free itself from man's body and world's time in order to mount to eternity. That ascent alone is the pilgrimage named so often in this play.

Patristic commentary on the master's journey can help explain another aspect of the play that exhibits a parallel richness of meaning. The action's place in historical time is allegorically as ambiguous as is the duration of the dying, and the play's movement from a double to a single *time* is one of its finest artistic strategies. Because the play concerns a single figure called Everyman—printed by Cawley, quite properly, as one word with a capital E—it speaks of death as it may come to any one of us, individually, at any time. The play's historical moment is in that sense a perpetual present, not tied down to history. But simultaneously a specific historical time is also addressed which is nothing less than Doomsday, the general death that will befall *all those* still living at the end of the world. We are implicated collectively as well as individually, for there is a steady, sustained ambivalence of pronoun in God's opening speech: Everyman is spoken of as both singular and plural in number.[20] I shall italicize the alternation:

> *Euery man* lyueth so after *his owne* pleasure,
> And yet of *theyr* lyfe *they* be nothynge sure.
> I se the more that I *them* forbere
> The worse *they* be fro yere to yere.
> *All that lyueth* appayreth faste;
> Therfore I wyll, in all the haste,
> Haue a rekenynge of *euery mannes* persone;
> For, and I leue *the people* thus alone
> In *theyr* lyfe and wycked tempestes,
> Veryly *they* will become moche worse than beestes,
> For now *one* wolde by enuy *another* vp ete;
> Charyte *they* do all clene forgete.
> I hoped well that *euery man*
> In my glory sholde make *his* mansyon,
> And therto I had *them* all electe.... (40-54)

When God gives His order to Dethe:

> Go thou to *Eueryman*
> And shewe *hym*, in my name,
> A pylgrymage *he* must on hym take, (66–68)

we seem to be safely back in the singular; but Dethe's answer again allows no one to escape:

> Lorde, I wyll in the worlde go renne ouer-all
> And cruelly out-serche *bothe grete and small*. (72-73)

The ambiguity is present even earlier in the opening speech of the Messenger, which denies the audience any certainty about the kind of death-and-judgment play they will see:

> For ye shall here how our Heuen Kynge
> Calleth Eueryman to a generall rekenynge. (19-20)

A listening audience cannot tell whether "Everyman" is written as one word or two, just as the word "general" can mean both "comprehensive" (a man giving a full account of his life) and "collective" (all men, the general) brought to judgment. The ambiguity is no accident: *I* do not know when I will die: *we* do not know when, as a race, we will have exceeded the patience of God.

The text provides for—indeed, subtly ensures—a kind of staging that will carry this meaning. The Messenger calls out from the *platea*: give audience to the play, hear what God has to say. God appears above to talk about *what He sees*—"euery man" in his sin—and for the first part of His speech at least, it seems clear that a character called Everyman should not be evident or distinguishable from the rest of the audience. The audience itself is the first "euery man" that God names: it is what is in His view, and what therefore He must be understood to order Dethe to summon. When Dethe cries "Loo, yonder I se Eueryman walkynge," "Eueryman, stande styll" (80, 85) the leading actor is designated, but until then he belongs in the audience, anonymous, unexceptional. The actor might well be directed to begin making his way easily and gracefully toward an exit just before the summons comes, for we live as though such matters hold no interest, cannot concern our own life. Only when Death names us directly do we take any notice, and then, like Everyman, bewildered and unready, it is in the broken rhythms of "What, sente to me?" Reluctantly Everyman will acknowledge that summons—up to this point ambiguous—in the name of us all, for he is at once our likeness and our brother.

Neither the *ars moriendi* nor the faithful-friend analogues can offer any explanation for this doubled pronoun of address, this dual sense of time. They concern a man's death, that is all. But the parable of the talents does exhibit this same allegorical doubling of significance. The man gone on a pilgrimage to a far country is Christ, and the parable speaks of what will be required when He returns, at the Second Coming, which is Doomsday. Gregory explains it so:

For when the judge will come, he will ask from each of us as much as he gave. Therefore, so that each one may be sure of giving a reckoning when the Lord returns, he should think fearfully every day of what he has received. For, lo, the day is near when he who went on a journey to a far land will return. For he who left this earth on which he was born did indeed as it were go away to a far country; but he will surely return, and demand a reckoning for the talents....[21]

This understanding of the parable's "moment" must be the source of the darker, more apocalyptic overtones of God's opening speech in the play. Until the very last of its forty-two lines there is no mention of death, nor of pilgrimage or journey, nor is any clear priority given the singular pronoun. We hear instead about sin, and justice, and a general reckoning. It is the language of the master returned. Only in the command given Dethe, at line 68, is it clear this play will concern a rehearsal of the Final Day, that its subject is that individual judgment at any individual death which will be formally recapitulated at the Day of Doom.[22]

These then are some ways in which attention to the parable can enable a closer and more accurate description of certain aspects of the play than has perhaps been readily available before. Let me choose just one more instance, last in my sequence, but far from least: the character and function of Good Dedes.

The problem is not one of any substantial misunderstanding. We see Good Dedes go into the grave with Everyman; we honor the fact that she alone does not desert him; and in a general sense, we understand why. But the parable of the talents can allow us to name that reason with greater precision. It seems likely Jerome's use of *opera* furnished her name, Good Dedes, but her specific *function* in the play derives from another part of the parable. She is the crucial part of the reckoning Everyman must make, the *spiritual profit*, the *increase*, which God demands of his servants when he calls back the talents and hears the accounts. The reckoning concerns *lucrum spirituale*, and the servant cast into exterior darkness is he who hides his talent in the earth, becoming thereby unprofitable in the economy of God's love and man's salvation. Good Dedes in the play, we may say simply and surely, is the profit on Everyman's total endowment: on his beauty, strength, reason, senses, friends, kindred, goods.

And in a manner again intrinsic to the parable—which speaks as though literal riches were its subject—the play creates a special relationship between Goodes and Good Dedes. There is on the one hand, however peculiar to the English language, the close verbal link between their names. And there is besides a close emblematic relationship. Both are initially discovered prostrate and unable to move: Goodes because it is stacked, trussed, locked in chests, sacked in bags (393-397), as a talent hoarded and hidden rather than put out for use; and Good Dedes because she is buried in earth ("Here I lye, colde in the grounde") and fettered by sin (486–488). These parallels suggest what the Fathers declare explicitly and what the play itself will later make clear: that the one must become the other; that goods (here standing in for all of the talents) must become good deeds.[23] Dethe, in his opening summary of what we will see, offers one of those synonyms so oddly characteristic of this play, giving a character a name other than that he ordinarily bears. Everyman will dwell in hell forever, he tells us, "Excepte that almes be his good frende" (78). Later, the play will explore in action the logic of that oblique naming. After Everyman has returned from Confession, he makes of his last will and testament his best Good Deed, adding to (and defining the nature of) those few earlier good deeds his penance has set free to walk again:

> Now herken, all that be here,
> For I wyll make my testament
> Here before you all present:

85

> In almes halfe my good I wyll gyue with my handes twayne
> In the way of charyte with good entent,
> And the other halfe styll shall remayne
> In queth, to be retourned there it ought to be. (696-702)

What is rightfully his—one half of his goods—he leaves to the poor in alms. What he has gained wrongfully—the other half—he will have restored to those he took from. He makes restitution, and he performs through his "almesse" the seven works of charity—those actions that alone can insure man's salvation at the Day of Doom, and which are named by Christ in the verses that immediately follow the parable of the talents in Matthew 25. They are those good deeds to the poor and wretched which cannot be done generously without doing them to Christ: "To fede the hungry; to gyf the thristy drynke; to clethe the nakyd; to herber the howsles; to viset the seke; to viset prisonners; to bery the dede."[24] Those deeds are the medieval meaning of "almesse," whether accomplished by one's own hand or by a legacy to the Church. "As long as you did it to one of these my least brethren, you did it to me" (Matthew 25:31-46). Everyman has come a long spiritual way from that earlier attempt to put his Goodes to use, when he sought to buy off Dethe for "a thousande pounde" (122).

This same passage affords a second instance of the way the parable of the talents, within medieval tradition, seems to have gathered to itself many like or nearby things. Everyman's last will and testament derives almost word–for–word from St. Luke's story of Zacheus, a rich man of Jericho and a sinner, in whose house Jesus announces He will stay. The respectable people murmur against it:

> But Zacheus, standing, said to the Lord: Behold, Lord, the half of my goods I give to the poor; and if I have wronged any man of any thing, I restore him fourfold.
>
> Jesus said to him: This day is salvation come to this house, because he also is a son of Abraham.
>
> For the Son of man is come to seek and to save that which was lost. (Luke 19:8-10)

The speech of Zacheus above must be the ultimate source of Every-

man's alms-giving and restitution, whatever medieval handbooks
for priests may stand between. This ultimate indebtedness, so far
as I know, has never been noted; but more interesting from our
present point of view is the fact that Luke's version of the talents
follows immediately.

Although in this play Confession is initially spoken of as a "clens-
ynge ryuere," a "gloryous fountayne" that can wash away sin (536,
545), the dialogue soon moves from that imagery into a long prayer
spoken by Everyman, rehearsing his sins and asking mercy (581-
618). (At the end of it, Good Dedes is at last enabled to move. *The
Book of Vices and Virtues*, a fourteenth-century English translation
of the immensely influential *Somme le Roi*, discusses the sacrament
of penance in ways helpful here and very closely related to the
parable of the talents. It says that man should think of his Holy
Confessor as God's Bailiff, conducting (and through the sacrament
clearing) a preliminary rendering of accounts, of all of our "re-
ceites" and "dispences."[25] Good Dedes, free to move, will carry the
account-book, for she is what it records:

> *Everyman*. Good Dedes, haue we clere our rekenynge?
> *Good Dedes*. Ye, in dede, I haue it here. (652-53)

It is now clarified by penance of all *except* good deeds—the spiritual
profit he will present as evidence of an (ultimately) faithful steward-
ship of talents entrusted for a time and now recalled. And in his
own hand, with equal symbolic force, Everyman bears the cross—
the sign of that one Good Deed man could not accomplish on his
own, sufficient to remedy Adam's sin. In two of the *Gesta Romanorum*
versions of the faithful friend story, the third friend (more commonly
identified as Good Deeds or Charity) is Christ himself, the friend
willing to die to prevent His friend's dying.[26] Without that sacrifice,
no account books kept on earth could ever win grace. V. Wyttes
notes this crucial fact after Everyman's visit to Priesthode for the
sacraments:

> Peas! For yonder I se Eueryman come,
> Whiche hath made true satysfaccyon. (769-770)

It names the change as though Everyman were its agent; but of course the facts are otherwise. Christ alone could make true satisfaction for sin—He is the great restitution—but it is available to any man through the sacrament of the altar. Everyman makes satisfaction in the only way possible for man fallen and forlorn: he satisfies justice by accepting Christ's body into his own. That assent and mystical incorporation win him heaven at the end. The third chapter of *The Boke of the Craft of Dying* advises as a medicine against despair that the dying man be helped to say:

The deth of oure lord Ihesu Crist I put betwene me and all myn euell meritis, and the merite of his worthi passione I offre for the merite that I shuld haue had and alas I haue it not; Sey also: Lord put the deth of oure lord Ihesu Criste betwene me and thi ryghtwysnes.[27]

From this medieval Christian truth derives the power of the penultimate stage image: Good Dedes and the accounts-book, Everyman and the cross of Christ. The union is emblematic. They go into the grave together, for the lack of either would destroy the hope of heaven. Having learned to wish to die, Everyman has learned the highest lesson of the art of dying well: "I go before there I wolde be. God be our gyde" (780). The play now moves swiftly to its end as all except Good Dedes fall away at the grave's edge. Everyman commends his soul to God, asks to be saved at the Day of Doom, and is received above to the sound of heavenly singing. An angel speaks to him, "Come, excellente electe spous, to Iesu!" It is equivalent to the parable's "Enter thou into the joy of thy lord."

All this would seem to indicate that some knowledge of the parable of the talents, and the commentary that grew up around it, can offer important help to our understanding of the play. For certain central facts, it has claim to be the necessary cause; and if that is granted, it becomes (in the technical sense) an adequate cause for other characters, events, and actions of the play. But the question of external probability remains. Evidence is needed that this Death-and-Doomsday subject was elsewhere and in important places conceived in terms of the parable of the talents: that the conjunction of the two would have seemed natural to a late fifteenth-century dramatist and readily comprehensible to some reasonable portion of his audience.

88

If space were available to sketch the history of the parable and its influence on medieval vernacular literature, one might wish to begin by looking at the *Bestiary* of Guillaume le Clerc, written in Anglo-Norman in 1210 or thereabouts, which uses the parable significantly; or at that same author's *Le Besant de Dieu*, where the talents provide the governing idea for the entire poem.[28] But later evidence will serve our present purposes better. The most important link between Doomsday and the parable of the talents in popular medieval tradition is the *Speculum humanae salvationis*—one of the most important books of the later Middle Ages, and (along with the *Biblia pauperum*) one of the two most popular versions of sacred history read as a series of typologically-related events. The *Speculum* was written in 1324, and was so widely disseminated that no census has ever been attempted of all of its surviving examples. (Lutz and Perdrizet, whose two-volume study[29] remains the most important work on the subject, knew of 205 Latin and Latin-German manuscripts, nearly 80 of them fully illustrated.) The text was translated into German, French, English, Dutch, and Czech. It became one of the most popular block-books, again with extant examples beyond numbering. Granted the close relationship that exists between *Everyman* and *Elckerlijc*, we might note the fact of translation into both English and Dutch; and we might recall as well that the Netherlands was a great center of block-book printing.

The *Speculum* concerns us because in it, the Last Judgment is prefigured by 1) the parable of the talents, 2) the parable of the wise and foolish virgins, and 3) the writing on the wall at Belshazzar's feast. In the block-books and the illuminated manuscripts, the four are most often depicted in a series spread across two pages, with their texts below and the Last Judgment at the extreme left.[30] Christ is seated on an arc in the heavens, displaying His wounds, the lily and a two-edged sword emerging from His mouth; Mary and John kneel on either side of Him, and the dead arise from their graves below. Directly alongside this picture is shown the parable of the talents, with the reckoning completed and the unprofitable servant bound and being led out to torture.[31] The influence of this work upon the visual arts was very considerable; it would have made the relationship I postulate between parable and play one that would have been more easily accessible to contemporary audiences (even the illiterate) than it is to us now. My evidence from the Fathers indicated that the parable was understood in terms of Doomsday. The present evidence makes it clear that the converse was also true, and *via* the block-books well into the sixteenth century: Doomsday was thought of in terms of the parable of the talents.

There are intermediate works that should be looked at in detail, but here can only be mentioned. A late fifteenth-century Scots poem, "The Thrie Tailes of the Thrie Priests of Peblis," offers evidence closely contemporary with *Everyman* that the talents-version of the crisis survived, even though many of the analogues in between name it only in a generalized way as "being in peril of death." The Scots poem, like these others, never uses the word "talents," but it does specify the precise reckoning required by the King of Kings (identified so in the tale's second line):

> Thus but [i.e., *without*] delay befoir him to compeir.
> And with him count and give reckning of all
> He had of him al tyme baith grit and smal.[32]

And from the fourteenth century in England, there is a remarkable example of all these traditions flourishing together, clustered around the idea of the talents. In one of the *Middle English Sermons* edited by Ross, there is narrated a version of the faithful-friend story that has never been formally noticed in *Everyman* criticism.[33] It is used as an exemplum on the theme *Redde quod debes*—"Yelde that thou owest"—but between the first statement of the text and the narration of the story there intervenes a most elaborate development of theme, subsidiary theme, and illustration. It demonstrates most vividly how the idea of the talents as such subsumed material from all three parables I spoke of earlier. One hears first of the unmerciful servant of Matthew 18, who owed a debt of ten thousand talents, after which the other parable of the talents is narrated. Luke is the version cited—quite properly, for the synonym "besauntes" is used for talents, and the unprofitable servant hides his talent in a napkin rather than the ground—but it details an unequal distribution of talents, using the 5-2-1 sequence Matthew's gospel alone provides. The preacher then goes on to quote the speech of Zacheus (again from Luke) that furnishes Everyman his last will and testament. He generalizes from it: "than it semeth well here-by that euery man is bondon to peye is dette of the goodes that God hath sende hym," and after speaking of alms-deeds and their necessity, he names Christ as man's ultimate and only way of settling his debt with God. The preacher then—and only then—goes on to narrate the story of the three friends, one of whom alone is faithful. There is no other text I know that shares so many of the materials the dramatist of *Everyman* used in his turn.

These intermediate links testify to the continuity of the tradition; and some later proof, of an oddly circumstantial kind, can take us further into the sixteenth century. Our text of *Everyman* depends chiefly upon two early editions printed by John Skot which survive complete. Two other editions, printed by Richard Pynson, are extant only in fragmentary form, one of them dated c. 1510-1525, and the other c. 1525-1530. The year 1525 links both guesses,[34] though guesses, of course, they remain. But it is interesting to find Pynson, in the following year, 1526, publishing a treatise called *The Pylgrimage of Perfection*, whose seventh chapter of the first book concerns God's gifts to man:

god wyll/that suche/gyftes & graces that he hath frely and without deseruyng gyuen to man/shuld nat be taken in vayn: but whan he cometh to the yeres of discrecion/& hath the vse of reason/he shuld labour and exercise hymselfe in them: for *they be the talentes* that god hath *lent* to man in this lyfe: of the whiche he wyll aske moste *streyt accounte* in the *daye of iudgement*....[35] [italics mine]

We have what I called earlier the essential verbal matrix of the play of *Everyman*, and (as with the Lydgate verses quoted then) one further word, "talents," which is the explanation of the rest. If *Everyman* was indeed written in the 1480's, this treatise is later by some forty years; but the printed editions (which are all that remain) testify at the very least to its popularity in the early decades of the sixteenth century. This evidence suggests that Richard Pynson, or anyone reading both of these works from his press, would surely have understood the parable of the talents to be the Scriptural text underlying *Everyman*. On the basis of evidence already put forward they would almost equally surely not have been the first to do so.

I have one final reason, perhaps stronger than the others, for this. As noted before, *Barlaam and Ioasaph*, a Greek work of the eleventh century, has long been recognized as the earliest source of the (Christianized) faithful-friend story, but since there are many intermediate versions of the same, *Everyman* scholarship has tended to concern itself with those that are later in time and nearer in place. This is quite proper: no one would wish to claim for the dramatist direct knowledge of an early Greek original. It was, indeed, the last version I turned to in my research. But it offers a most striking confirmation of the reading I had reached (and have so far been putting forward) on other grounds. For the Fifth Apologue of that work, the ultimate source of our story, names the crisis confronting the man who had three friends in this way:

Now one day he was apprehended by certain dread and strange soldiers, that made speed to hale him to the king, there to render account for a debt of ten thousand talents [Ταλάντων].

In the end it is only the neglected third friend,

the company of good deeds,—faith, hope, charity, alms, kindliness, and the whole band of virtues, that can go before us, when we quit the body, and may plead with the Lord on our behalf, and deliver us from our enemies and dread creditors, who urge that strict rendering of account in the air. . . .[36]

In short, the story which gives to *Everyman* its most distinctive action and shape—the testing of friends—in its earliest Christian version explicitly works from the idea of the talents. The Greek author takes the figure ten thousand from Matthew 18: it makes a striking beginning, and all preliminaries can be avoided by simply announcing a call to repay a huge debt. But Matthew 18 contributes nothing except that specific number. For the rest, we are dealing with the meaning of the talents as defined by those several centuries of patristic commentary on Matthew 25 that preceded this eleventh-century narrative. Without that implicit

92

understanding of what the debt involves, "the company of good deeds" and "the whole band of virtues" would make no sense as a way of explaining the third and faithful friend.

Should there be any doubt that the Scriptural sense of "talent" is alive in his pages, the author's introduction to the whole work can put it to rest:

So I too...heedful of the danger hanging over that servant who, having received of his lord the talent, buried it in the earth, and hid out of use that which was given him to trade withal, will in no wise pass over in silence the edifying story that hath come to me....It readeth thus.[37]

The Jesuit scholar, Jean Sonet, in a recent two-volume study of *Barlaam and Ioasaph* and its transmission, names a normative medieval Latin version, of which sixty-two manuscripts are known to him: its features include both the debt of ten thousand talents and praise of the third friend as returning *with usury* (that is, with spiritual profit) such small kindness as had been shown him.[38] Again, the second of these details makes sense only in relation to the later parable. It cannot derive from Matthew 18.

Whether the talents survive as an explicit detail in any given version, or whether they have gone underground, as in the *Golden Legend*, here translated by Caxton,

And it happed so that this man was in grete perylle of his lyf and was somoned tofore the kynge,[39]

in either case it seems clear that this parable continued to be the explanation of that action and its deepest controlling logic, from the eleventh century well into the sixteenth.

What happens on stage in no way *looks like* visual representations of the parable as they are found, say, in the *Speculum humanae salvationis*, where it is usual for two servants to be shown presenting coins or purses, while the third is bound and punished.[40] Instead the stage is occupied by allegorical personages who are explicitly, denotatively, what those coins signify, with Everyman and his account-books at their center. He is engaged in a different literal action—the testing of friends—with the result that the symbols and referents of the parable have perforce been recombined, shaped into something new, and no single patristic commentary has been used with perfect consistency or as a whole. But Everyman offers in reckoning still his Good Dedes and the cross of Christ. We know that the first Christian redactor of that testing-of-friends story had the talents in mind; they were his reason for telling it, and determined its moral. When a version of that story, probably not much longer than its original, came into the hands of a fifteenth-century dramatist, the parable and its commentaries seem once again to have provided clues and indications as to how that brief exemplum might be expanded into a complex work of art. His procedures were eclectic, certainly. His concern was to make a play potent to move a popular audience, not to transmit lecture notes on the Fathers; and so he used what seemed useful, governed only by the need to make of those old materials something strong and stageable and new, at once dramatically coherent and doctrinally correct.

We do not see the parable staged, but unless we would ignore the fact that ideas have histories and that drama involves words spoken— uses words because it is interested in ideas more complex than dumb shows can manage—then we may find that the text that lies behind this play is like the soil beneath a rich carpet of green grass: it has a great deal to do with everything we do see that is substantial, pleasing, and alive. And it can help us see it better, for it invites a closer attention to the actual language of the play, permits a more precise definition of what is underway at any given moment, and—not least—allows us to apprehend more clearly the play's essential unity of action.

For modern audiences, *Everyman* is perhaps most moving, most successful, in its "tragic" action—its imitation of how a man dies. We are more than ever in search of an *ars moriendi*, having abandoned the medieval kind. But the other part of the play, its rising action—that which moves toward joy and reconciliation and salvation—has its own power and special conviction still, if only because once that was where the deepest truth was known to reside. For a medieval audience this "play of holy dying" was most urgently a play about holy living, an *ars vivendi atque moriendi*. The parable of the talents in no small part was responsible for that.

NOTES

1. A. C. Cawley, ed., *Everyman* (Manchester, 1961); hereafter cited as "Cawley." All references to the play are to this edition. The possible priority of the Dutch *Elckerlijc* over the English *Everyman* is of no real consequence to this paper, and I have not thought it necessary to rehearse that problem here. If *Everyman* is indeed a translation from the Dutch, it is a fully achieved translation; its audiences would not have been aware they were watching a foreign play. I am concerned with the meaning of the action and the words which describe it for an English audience.

2. For "rekenynge," see ll. 20, 70, 99, 106, 113, 137, 147, 160, 333, 375, 419, 511, 529, 652, 865, 914; for "accounte," ll. 244, 336, 376, 406, 420, 493, 551, 580, 916. And cf. "my wrytynge" in l. 187.

3. Cawley's note to l. 104 (p. 31) relates such language to the verses on the bailiff in Lydgate's translation of the French *Dance of Death* poem. But there, terms such as "assise," "sommened," "to yefe a-comptes," are used simply as a witty play on the bailiff's own profession. It is too particular, and too late in date, to offer a source for this kind of language. See *The Dance of Death*, ed. Florence Warren, with an introduction by Beatrice White, *EETS*, o.s. 181 (London, 1931): 36 [Ellesmere MS version].

4. Minor devils were sometimes thought of as recording man's sins, sometimes in a slightly comic context, as in the Doomsday pageant of *The Towneley Plays*, ed. George England and Alfred W. Pollard, *EETS*, e.s. 71 (London, 1897): 371–79; or in exempla concerning St. Brice (for several references, see V. A. Kolve, *The Play Called Corpus Christi* [Stanford, 1966], p. 140 and p. 299, n. 43). More often, this is treated gravely, as in the *ars moriendi* block-book illustration of how dying men may be tempted to despair. It shows a devil at the deathbed, holding up a large bill-of-writing and a scroll which says *Ecce peccata tua*. See the facsimile *ars moriendi*, ed. W. Harry Rylands, Holbein Society (London, 1881 [no pagination]). The drama's Everyman must present *his own* account-book; it is a different tradition altogether.

5. See also ll. 57, 437–41. Words signifying something "lent" occasionally occur in connection with the fifth temptation named by the *ars moriendi*, that of family and temporal things. See, for instance, *Ratis Raving and Other Moral and Religious Pieces*, ed. J. Rawson Lumby, *EETS*, o.s. 43 (London, 1870): 5–6. But this most probably derives *from* the parable of the talents, and should not be regarded as an ultimately independent source.

6. Henry Noble MacCracken, ed., *The Minor Poems of John Lydgate, Part I*, *EETS*, e.s. 107 (London, 1911): 337 (217–24).

7. For an introduction and bibliographical guide to the literature of the *ars moriendi*, see Sister Mary Catharine O'Connor, *The Art of Dying Well* (New York, 1942).

95

8. See *The Homilies of S. John Chrysostom . . . on the Gospel of St. Matthew, Part III*, trans. Sir George Prevost (London, 1885), pp. 1041–42; cf. also pp. 1027–28. Chrysostom died in 407.

9. In *Patrologiae cursus completus: Patrologia Latina*, ed. J.P. Migne, 221 vols, Paris, 1844–1864, hereafter cited as *P.L.* For Rabanus Maurus, *Commentariorum in Matthaeum* (written c. 822–826) , see vol. 107, col. 1095.

10. Gregory the Great (c. 540–604), *XL Homiliarum in Evangelia*, *P.L.* 76, col. 1109.

11. Chrysostom, op. cit., pp. 1041–42.

12. For the pseudo-Bede, see *In Matthaei Evangelium Expositio*, *P.L.* 92, col. 109. Paul the Deacon (c. 720–800) in his *Homiliarius*, *P.L.* 95, cols. 1554–55, lays distinctive emphasis on skills in the various arts and crafts. For the *Glossa Ordinaria*, see *P.L.* 114, col. 166.

13. Hilary of Poitiers (c. 315–367), *Commentarius in Matthaeum*, *P.L.* 9, cols. 1061–63.

14. Rabanus Maurus, *De universo* (c. 844), *P.L.* 111, col. 79.

15. St. Jerome (c. 342–420), *Commentaria in Evangelium S. Matthaei*, *P.L.* 26, col. 186. In the pseudo-Jerome *Expositio Quatuor Evangeliorum: Matthaeus*, *P.L.* 30, col. 559, the endowments are distinguished less clearly: *quinque sensus, intellectus et operatio, intellectus* alone. For Isidore (c. 560–636), see *P.L.* 83, col. 124, and for Rabanus, see *P.L.* 111, col. 79. They both offer the Five Books–Two Testaments–Grace interpretation as well.

16. Lawrence V. Ryan, in a distinguished essay, "Doctrine and Dramatic Structure in *Everyman*", *Speculum* 32 (1957), 722–35, addresses this question among others, and makes a strong case for the "acknowledge" interpretation. But I take the fact that the word appears only as noun or proper name to be crucial; in that form, and in the absence of contextual limitation, it is unlikely to have been understood as "acknowledgement". Note too that Knowledge is introduced to Everyman in response to his request for "counseyll" (516) ; later he asks to be given "cognycyon" (538) about where to go to Confession. Knowledge is the answer to both, and would seem to be synonymous with them. See Helen S. Thomas, "The Meaning of the Character Knowledge in 'Everyman,' " *Mississippi Quarterly* 14 (1961), 3–13, for a summary (with full references) of scholarship devoted to this problem, and a useful contribution to it. She also concludes, for reasons other than those outlined above, that Knowledge is a "Wisdom-figure."

17. See ll. 732, 737–39, on the need to go beyond sense evidence.

18. For "pylgrymage," see ll. 68, 146, 331, 550, 565, 629, 673, 784, 818; for "journey," ll. 103, 141, 242, 247, 259, 268, 279, 295, 363, 464, 495, 641; for "vyage," ll. 415, 674, 782. At l. 566, Penance is described briefly as "this vyage," and an awkward parallel construction at ll. 141–142 can be easily misread; but the subject everywhere else is unequivocally the soul-journey.

19. Rev. Josiah Forshall and Sir Frederic Madden, eds., *The Holy Bible . . .*

made from the Latin Vulgate by John Wycliffe and his Followers, 4 vols. (Oxford, 1850), 4, pp. 70–71, 210–211.

20. See R. W. Zandvoort, "Everyman–Elckerlijc," *Etudes Anglaises* 6 (1953): 1–15.

21. Gregory the Great, loc. cit.

22. See Cawley's note to l. 885. Ll. 259–261 confirm that Doomsday is not yet, but to come.

23. See especially ll. 431–34. Cf. "A Poem of Goods," ed. A.G. Rigg, *A Glastonbury Miscellany of the Fifteenth Century*, Oxford, 1968, pp. 65–66.

24. British Museum MS. Add. 37049, fol. 55, names them so on a tree of the works of mercy. (It is an English miscellany from the first half of the fifteenth century.) The Doomsday plays of the Corpus Christi cycles stage an enquiry into these deeds as their major action.

25. W. Nelson Francis, ed., *The Book of Vices and Virtues*, EETS, o.s. 217, (London, 1942): 174. Also of interest are pp. 68–92, 212–15.

26. S.J.H. Herrtage, ed., *The Early English Versions of the Gesta Romanorum*, ed. *EETS*, e.s. 33 (London, 1879): 131–132. Lines 778–80 make it clear that Everyman now bears in his hands a cross.

27. "The Boke of the Craft of Dying," in *Yorkshire Writers: Richard Rolle... and his Followers*, ed. Carl Horstmann, 2 vols. (London, 1895, 1896), 2, 413.

28. For the *Bestiaire*, see the edition by Robert Reinsch (Leipzig, 1890), p. 374 [1. 3469 ff.], or the translation by George Claridge Druce (Ashford, Kent, 1936), p. 94 ff. For the *Besant Dieu*, see the edition by Ernest E. Martin (Halle, 1869). "Besant" derives from the Latin *bysantium*, meaning a Byzantine coin; the Wycliffite Bible uses it as an English synonym for "talent" as well. On these works by Guillaume, see M. Dominica Legge, *Anglo-Norman Literature and its Background* (Oxford, 1963), pp. 207–8, 228–29.

29. J. Lutz and P. Perdrizet, eds., *Speculum Humanae Salvationis*, 2 vols. (Mulhouse, 1907, 1909). They name Matthew 25 as being the text most important to the passage, while noting that "*dans Luc les talents deviennent des mines. C'est de mines que parle le* Speculum" (1, 233), For the Latin text, see 1, 82; for the French translation made by Jean Mielot in 1448, see 1, 156–57. On the Dutch translations, see 1, 104. A fifteenth-century English translation was edited by Alfred H. Huth for the Roxburghe Club, vol. 118 (London, 1888), as *The Miroure of Mans Salvacionne;* see pp. 137–38. M. R. James and Bernard Berenson edited a facsimile-volume of a fourteenth-century Italian manuscript, *Speculum Humanae Salvationis* (Oxford, 1926), with valuable introductions. Other facsimile editions have been made by J. Ph. Berjeau (London, 1861), and by Ernst Kloss, 2 vols. (Munich, 1925).

30. See the Kloss facsimile, p. 62.

31. Its text is based on the Luke version of the parable, but it has on either side of it pictures and texts that name Matthew 25 as their source; and sometimes, as in Pierpont Morgan MS. 385, a fifteenth-century Dutch manuscript, Matthew

25 and Luke 19 are *both* named as sources to the Talents pictures. Elsewhere, as in the Dutch block-book edited in facsimile by Kloss, Matthew 18, Matthew 25, and Apocalypse 20 are named as sources to the first two pictures, without Luke 19 being named at all. Luke is correctly cited more often than not, but this is evidence again of all three parables being treated almost as though they were one.

32. In David Laing, *Early Popular Poetry of Scotland and the Northern Border*, ed. W. C. Hazlitt (London, 1895), 1, 159 (11. 1032–34); see also 11. 1104–05 and 1179–80. For later uses of the talents in poetry, see, e.g., Milton's sonnet on his blindness, and Dr. Johnson's verses "On the Death of Mr. Robert Levet."

33. Cawley, p. xix, discusses one analogue in *Middle English Sermons*, ed. W. O. Ross, *EETS*, o.s. 209 (London, 1940): 86 ff, but not the one on 36 ff, which I describe here. Ross's list of analogues is in a note to this first version, and since Cawley directs the reader to that list, it seems unlikely he overlooked it entirely.

34. See Cawley, p. ix.

35. *The Pylgrimage of Perfection*, printed by Richard Pynson, 1526, S.T.C. 3277, p. 20v. Wynkyn de Worde also published the work in 1531, S.T.C. 3278, pp. 12–12v.

36. [St. John Damascene], *Barlaam and Ioasaph*, ed. and trans. G.R. Woodward and H. Mattingly (Loeb Classical Library, 1914; reprinted with an introduction by David Marshall Lang, 1967), pp. 192–99. The attribution of authorship to St. John Damascene has been discredited. For a detailed study of the history of this fascinating work, see Lang's introduction to his translation of a Georgian version of the same, *The Wisdom of Balahvar* (London, 1957), pp. 11–65.

37. *Barlaam and Ioasaph*, p. 5.

38. Jean Sonet, S.J., *Le Roman de Barlaam et Josaphat*, 2 vols. (Namur and Paris, 1949, 1950), 1, 37–40, 74–88.

39. Quoted by Cawley, p. xviii.

40. The works cited in n. 29 name and/or reproduce a good many illustrations to the parable. Some others I have seen in manuscript are perhaps worth listing: Bodley MS. Laud Misc. 165, fol. 399v and fol. 460v (William of Nottingham's Commentary on the Gospels); Bodley MS. Douce 204, fol. 40 (a *Speculum*); British Museum MS. Royal 15 D. v., fol. 173 (Gregory's Homilies); and four MSS. of the *Speculum* at the Pierpont Morgan Library: MS. M. 140, fol. 42v; MS. M. 385, fol. 42; MS. M. 766, fol. 61v; MS. M. 782, fol. 74.

THE STAGING OF SAINT PLAYS IN ENGLAND

Glynne Wickham

I

HISTORIANS like categorizing. And who is to deny the propriety of their siftings of evidence, separating fact from fiction, relating consequences to actions and *vice-versa?* Yet to admit this does not preclude our taking note of the dangers implicit in this predilection for categories, most importantly that of explaining events in terms of cause and effect. Anyone who has read the exposure of the fallacies of the evolutionary approach to the history of medieval drama set out in the opening pages of O.B. Hardison's *Christian Rite and Christian Drama*[1] needs no further warning of what these dangers are.

I would like to start this essay, therefore, by extending this object-lesson of Hardison's to that part of the evolutionary explanation of dramatic development which relates to Saint Plays. Orthodox histories of English drama have normally categorized plays relating to the lives of saints and martyrs as relatively late developments in point of historical chronology and, on this account, as "extensions" or "offshoots" of the vernacular mystery cycles and morality plays which had preceded them.* An implication of this argument is that

_____

* For an exception see Professor Ten Brink's opinion quoted on p. 101, below.

because this type of play appears so late and thus so near the close of this epoch and the eclipse of religious drama, it must necessarily have been insignificant. Certainly none of the several types of drama popular in the Middle Ages has attracted less attention from theatre historians and critics of literature.

One explanation of this situation, of course, is the relative paucity of texts surviving for study; another is the obvious association (in Protestant and Humanist minds following the Reformation) of plays devoted to the miracles of obscure saints with the worst excesses of Roman Catholic superstition and idolatry. Even a reading of those plays which do survive does not encourage active revival, at least at first glance: verse which is bad when it is not indifferent, cast lists which are long when they are not numerically defeating, and stage directions prescribing conflagrations, massacres, and cures which tax the ingenuity of skilled technicians are the common characteristics of such plays, in England as elsewhere in Europe.

The temptation, then, to leave this "category" of play undisturbed is great and understandable, but I think we must resist it if we are to probe beneath surface appearances and to try to understand what made this type of play so attractive to its contemporaries. This reflection itself poses a question of some importance. Who were its contemporaries? Men and women of the early sixteenth or the late fifteenth century? This, certainly, is what orthodox literary discussions of such plays would lead us to believe. The evidence of the surviving English texts does nothing to discourage this idea. There are only three of them, excluding the plays of St. Anne and St. Veronica incorporated respectively in *Ludus Coventriae* and the Cornish cycle: the two plays in the Digby manuscript—St. Paul and Mary Magdalene—and the Cornish play of St. Meriasek. The Digby pair are usually dated by English scholars around the turn of the century; the date of the Cornish play is specified in the manuscript as 1504. Yet hints have been appearing in recent years to warn us against too ready an acceptance of so circumscribed a dating of this genre. There is Carleton Brown's "An Early Mention of a St. Nicholas Play in England" in *Studies in Philology*, 38 (1931),[2]

Otto Pacht's *The Rise of Pictorial Narrative in Twelfth Century England* (1962),[3] and Harbage and Schoenbaum's *Annals of English Drama, 907-1700* (1964)[4] to awaken us to other possibilities. Even a careful reading of Appendix W and Appendix X in E.K. Chamber's *The Medieval Stage*, published more than half a century ago, leads in this same direction; for this shows Saint Plays to have been ubiquitous and much longer lived than is generally allowed.

Let us take the time span first. References to a play of St. Katherine in London in 1393, and to a play of St. Thomas the Martyr at King's Lynn in Norfolk in 1385, take us back to Wyclif's strictures on miracle plays and to Chaucer's Wife of Bath with her visits "to pleyes of myracles and to mariages." As Chaucer states specifically that his Wife of Bath made these visits "in Lent," the plays in question can neither have been liturgical music-dramas nor Corpus Christi cycles. If Carleton Brown's thesis is accepted, we have to leap back a further hundred years to a St. Nicholas play in the middle of the thirteenth century. Further authority for doing this comes from the late twelfth century in Fitzstephen's reference to plays at Skinner's Well in London: "London has a more holy type of performance: representatives of the miracles which holy saints performed or of the sufferings by which the steadfastness of the martyrs became renowned."[5]

If, at the other end of our time-scale we take the play of St. Eustace at Braintree in Essex (1534?) and that of St. Thomas the Apostle at York in 1535 to have been among the last, we at once find ourselves confronted with a life span of three centuries, longer in fact than that of the Corpus Christi cycles or the moralities. And then, of course, if one wished to be really naughty, one might argue by the yardstick of the evolutionary hypothesis that Saint Plays were the parents and not the children of the mysteries and moralities! This is not quite as fantastic as it may sound, since it supplies grounds for believing that Professor Ten Brink may have been near to the truth when he suggested seventy years ago that "legendary subjects prepared the way for Biblical; scenes from the Old Testament for similar ones from the New; and so, finally, the most sacred portions of the story of salvation came to be represented openly."[6]

Another element of the pattern suggested by the references is the range and number of saints whose lives were recreated in dramatic form. These include not only such obvious names and familiar figures as St. George, St. Katherine, and St. Lawrence who constantly appear in glass, fresco and narrative painting, but also such obscure figures as Saint Crytyan, St. Sylvester and St. Meriasek who are as unfamiliar to us as the three martyrs, Félicien, Séverin and Exupère (the *Trois Doms* of the French "Mystère" of that name, which was written and performed at Romans in 1509).

Yet another feature of the pattern is the association in the records of plays performed in summer months with fields, and of plays performed in winter months with churches. Although by no means constant, this feature is striking enough in its recurrence to suggest a marked degree of expediency in the minds of the begetters of these plays, where choice of stage and auditorium was concerned. In Norwich and Lincoln, for example, Saint Plays were performed at Whitsuntide. July was the month chosen at Bethersden in Kent in 1522 for a play about St. Christina, and July was similarly favored by players at Bassingbourne in Cambridgeshire who presented a play about St. George of a very elaborate and costly nature in a field with a croft or barn. Canterbury preferred a pageant-wagon for its play of Thomas à Becket from 1504 onwards and used boy-actors. Actors in Coventry, however, used "the little Park" for their plays of St. Katherine in 1490 and St. Crytyan in 1504. Players at Braintree in Essex on the other hand used their Church for their plays of St. Swithin and St. Andrew in 1523 and 1525, as did most of the players in London in the fifteenth and sixteenth centuries who concerned themselves with Saint Plays.

In all of this there is a strong patronal element, which of itself advises us that local conditions were always likely to play a more important part than either doctrinal or diocesan considerations in the choice of subject and in the literary and theatrical treatment accorded to it. A particularly important aspect of this patronal element is the perennial need to raise funds to meet Church expenses.

A final deduction that I think one may draw from the references

I hope, however, I have said enough to establish grounds for approaching the subject of Saint Plays in a manner that is both more open-minded and more searching than most of us have had inclination to do hitherto.

II

I will begin this reappraisal then with one or two observations of a general nature about Saint Plays, based solely on the references to the English ones that have come to the notice of scholars up till now. Enough of these survive to reveal a pattern of sorts. The first pointer to this national pattern to strike my eye was the abruptness, coincident with Henry VIII's break with Rome, with which references to this type of play disappear. This suggests that the first fury of reformist-iconoclasts was directed against this sort of play, just as in the area of the fine arts it was directed against images of saints in sculpture and stained glass. This is something one might expect; what is surprising—at least it is to me in my reading of the general progress of stage censorship after 1531—is the nation-wide effectiveness of the ban on these plays. A hint of the possible reason for this is supplied in a letter from Henry VIII to his magistrates in York in 1535 or shortly after:

Whereas we understand by certain report of late evil and seditious rising in our ancient city of York, at the acting of a religious interlude of St. Thomas the Apostle, made in the same city on the 23rd. August now last past; and whereas we have been credibly informed that the said rising was owing to the seditious conduct of certain papists who took part in preparing for the said interlude, we will and require you that from henceward ye do your utmost to prevent and hinder any such commotion in future, and for this ye have my warrant for apprehending and putting in prison any papists who shall, in performing interludes which are founded on any portion of the Old or New Testament, say or make use of any language which may tend to excite those who are beholding the same to any breach of the peace.[7]

This letter supplies a good idea of the incendiary nature of Saint Plays at a time when matters of religious contention had become questions of political concern.

above—though perhaps with more hesitancy—is that Saint Plays presented at summer festivals in the open air were both costly and spectacular. Twenty-seven villages combined to meet the production costs of the St. George play at Bassingbourne in 1511. At Lincoln an inventory survives of the elaborate scenic properties required for the play of Tobias performed in 1564 and again in 1567 at the Broadgate. *Tobias* is a very late play and not, strictly speaking, a Saint Play at all but a biblical one; yet the scenic requirements so closely resemble in scale, quality and nature, those needed for the *Mystère des Trois Doms* at Romans in 1509, of which we have a complete record of costs, as to merit comparison. Nevertheless, with full allowance made for scholarly caution, collation of the surviving references to Saint Plays in England suffices of itself to explode the old categorizing of such plays as a by-product or late development of mysteries and moralities which, because all religious plays were by then in any case in full decline, can safely be ignored.

III

We can now turn our attention to the three surviving English texts—*St. Paul, St. Mary Magdalene* and *St. Meriasek,* and here the internal evidence which we possess at no point contradicts, and at many points confirms, the general deductions I have ventured to make this far. Of these three, *St. Meriasek* was unquestionably devised for production in the open air and in the round. The manuscript, like that of the Cornish Mysteries, is provided with diagrams of the round itself and the placement upon its circumference of the scaffolds or "stages" for the principal characters. Performance of *St. Meriasek* covered two days and the same scaffolds are adapted to the respective needs of the two parts of the play (fig. 1). For example, the scaffold required for King Conan on Day One is allotted to King Massen on Day Two (King Massen does not appear on Day One, nor King Conan on Day Two). Where characters appear on both days they retain the same scaffolds—the Emperor Constantine, the Bishop of Kernou, the Torturers, Heaven, and Hell. On Day One the center of the arena is

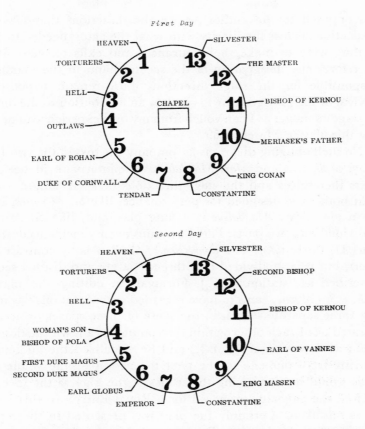

Fig. 1. Ground plans, from the original manuscript, for the staging of *St. Meriasek*: the arrangements of the scaffolds for the first day (*above*) and for the second day (*below*).

Reproduced by Whitley Stokes in his edition of the play, pp. 145 and 267.

occupied by a Chapel, but on Day Two it is empty. Some caution is needed in approaching the stage directions as these are added in a different (but contemporary) hand in the manuscript. My own guess is that this second hand is that of the producer or the director (as opposed to the author), since the directions themselves are indicative of close familiarity with what the actors needed to know, if they were to make their entrances and exits on cue. While, therefore, any designation of the second hand in the manuscript responsible for the stage directions must remain hypothetical, revival of the play goes far to confirm an attribution to the director or stage-manager as I can vouch from my own experience of producing this play in March 1969.

No such obliging diagrams accompany the text of the two Digby plays of *St. Paul* and *Mary Magdalene*. The internal evidence of the texts themselves and the stage-directions make it almost certain that both were designed for performance, like *St. Meriasek*, in the open air. *Mary Magdalene* is a long play and, like *St. Meriasek*, is divided into two parts: Part I contains twenty incidents or scenes, Part II, thirty-two. The *Conversion of St. Paul* is by contrast quite short, but it is subdivided into three separate and distinct sections described as "stations." F.J. Furnivall in editing the play for *E.E.T.S.* (1896), seems to have regarded these "stations" as meaning three separate stages, in the sense of three spaces or areas separated from each other within the confines of a town (he describes them as "open sites" [p. ix]), and he visualized the audience as moving from one site to the next to encompass the whole play. This would mean viewing the scenes of the play as the sovereign viewed the pageants prepared for a Royal Entry. In this I think he is mistaken. Certainly the play was presented in three parts, but it seems much more likely to me that the three scenes were brought before a single audience on pageant-wagons, one following in the wake of the other in the manner of the York and Chester Corpus Christi Cycles. In other words, "station" must be interpreted here as meaning the pageant-wagon and not the *platea* itself. The crux of the matter rests in our reading of lines 155 to 168 and the Latin stage-direction that lies between the last stanza of the first section and the first stanza of the second.

The lines which have caused the confusion are these:

ffynally of this stacon thus we mak a conclusyon,
besechyng thys audyens to follow and succede

with all your delygens this generall processyon,
To understande this matter wo lyst to rede
The holy bybyll for the better spede;
Ther shall he have the perfyth intellygens,
And thus we comyt you to crystys magnyfycens.

ffinis Istius stacionis, et altera sequitur.

The ambiguity lies in the Epilogue's two phrases, "besechyng thys audyens to folow and succede," and "this generall processyon." First, however, it should be noted that the whole of the Epilogue is optional, *"Poeta—si placet,"* and can be cut if desired. Secondly, the Latin stage direction at the close is in the singular: it is the second pageant, *altera*, which follows (*sequitur*), not the audience. Thirdly, there is no exhortation to the audience "to follow and succeed" at the end of the second pageant, and the stage direction is again in the singular: *ffinis istius secunde stacionis et sequitur tarcia.* Lastly, the word "processyon" may here mean no more than process in its legal or utilitarian sense; it just happens to scan better. What, then, the poet is exhorting the audience to follow is the rest of the story, which is both intelligible and important because it is taken directly from the Bible and will be communicated to those who attend diligently to the other pageants which will follow in due course. Anyone who is skeptical about this argument and regards it as special pleading should read the second stanza of the play (ll. 8-14) , where the same sentiments are couched in much the same words as the ambiguous lines 155 to 161, and where the word "proces," not "processyon" is used.

If this be granted, the ordering of the production becomes both clear and relatively simple. The play starts with a prayer spoken by the Poet/Prologue. Silence is thus obtained. The first pageant represents Saul as the chief persecutor of Christians in Jerusalem, about to set out for Damascus. "Here entryth Saule, goodly besene in the best wyse lyke an av(e)nterous Knyth." It consists of a cart of eight characters (including the Poet/Prologue/Epilogue), and represents either the temple or a council chamber for the Jewish elders in Jerusalem. In short, it is a Jerusalem-cart. At line 84 Saul, his servant and two soldiers step down from the pageant onto the *platea* and summon the Ostler, who is looking after some horses nearby. At line 126 the horses are brought out onto the *platea;* Saul and his escorts mount the horses during the next fifteen lines and are then ready to fulfil the stage direction: "Here Saule rydeyth forth with hys servantes about the place (and) owt of the pl(ace)." With Saul going off in one direction, Caiaphas, Annas, and the Poet are given sufficient lines (21) for the horsemen to get out of sight before the pageant-wagon itself moves off and the second pageant-wagon arrives to replace it. After seven introductory lines, Saul and his servants ride back into the place.

The new pageant represents Heaven and contains an entirely new cast of three (or four?) characters—Christ, an Angel, Ananias, and (?) the Holy Ghost. This pageant contains sufficient machinery to simulate thunder and lightning by means of which Saul's horse is made to throw him. Saul (now blinded) is taken by the soldiers to the side of the *platea*, where they stay in obscurity for thirty seven lines while Christ talks to Ananias. The soldiers are given thirteen lines between themselves to cover Ananias' descent from the pageant and to allow him to cross the *platea* to Saul. The baptism follows and the second pageant ends. Again the word "stacion" is used in the epilogue, and again it means the pageant-wagon itself. As it goes off, it is replaced either by a third wagon, or by a reappearance of the first pageant, "thys pageant at thys lytyll stacion" (1. 363). Here the ambiguity of the concluding lines of the first pageant is present once more; for, at face value, the word "pageant" may be interpreted to mean "the tableau," and the word "station" to mean the *platea* in which it is situated. A little reflection, however, cautions one against this reading of the line. In the first place neither Saul nor his soldiers have left that part of the original *platea* representing Damascus—at least there is no stage-direction to that effect—and the soldiers address the occupants of the third pageant within six lines of its arrival. Saul's last lines at the end of the second pageant are addressed to Ananias.

> Go forth yowur way; I will succede
> Into what place ye wyll me lede.   (11. 344-45)

I read this to mean that they depart from the *platea*—Ananias for good, and Saul to a convenient tiring house to change his costume. He has a hundred and fifty lines before returning "in a disciplis wede" (1. 502). The soldiers do not leave with Saul and Ananias, but re-mount their horses and go to greet Caiaphas in the newly arrived third pageant.

A second point to be noted is that the *platea* for the third pageant must be as large as that for the two preceding pageants, if only because of the nature of the action. It has to do duty for a diablerie as well as the temple in Jerusalem and the house in Damascus where Saul is hiding. Thus if this "pageant" and this "station" are both described as "little," we must take heed lest this be simply due to the poet's need to fill out this line and preserve his metre; they may not be intended to be taken literally. The text itself confirms this surmise.

The third section starts with a fifty-line section in Jerusalem to which the soldiers have returned. This is followed by a hundred-line interpolated scene among devils from Hell who erupt upon the *platea* and disappear again. Saul, still in Damascus, then preaches a sermon, his recent conversion symbolized by his change of costume. Attention then reverts to Caiaphas and Annas back in Jerusalem who lay a plot to destroy Saul. In Damascus Saul is warned of this by an Angel and plans to escape. A hymn, *Exultet celum laudibus*, brings the play to an end.

It will thus be observed that this third pageant is anything but "little," and that the *platea* is stretched to its fullest capacity. Indeed, I cannot myself see how this section of the play can be acted unless both the first and the second pageant wagon remain in the *platea;* if that is allowed, all problems relating to the staging of the play vanish at once. The Heaven-pageant (part II) provides the thunder that both escorts the devils on and off the stage and also the Angel in the third section. In the Caiaphas-Jerusalem pageant the actor who plays Saul's servant in section one doubles as the priests's servant in section three.

On this basis, the staging of the whole play takes the following form (see fig. 2). The audience is assembled in a town square around an open *platea:* on one side of the square is a coaching hotel.

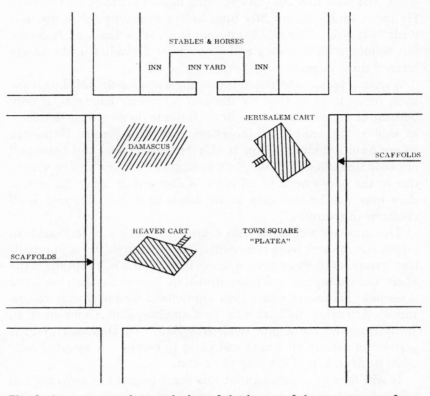

Fig. 2. A reconstructed ground plan of the layout of the town square for a performance of *The Digby Play of St. Paul*.

Into the *platea* comes the Poet aboard the Jerusalem-wagon. As he completes the Prologue, Saul enters independently from the direction of the hotel, dressed like a tyrant. After intimidating the audience, he crosses to the Jerusalem pageant and goes up into it. He collects letters from Annas and then descends to the *platea* again accompanied by a servant and two Knights. The servant hails the Ostler in the direction of the hotel and, after some buffoonery between the pair, horses are provided. Saul and the soldiers mount the horses, parade round the square, and depart while the Jerusalem-cart moves away from the center to the side of the square. These movements (and possibly a dance) give the cue for the entry into the *platea* of the Heaven-pageant, always supposing that it didn't enter together with the first one. The poet-author provides continuity. Saul and the Knights re-enter the platea; Saul is struck by lightning and blinded. His horse is quickly disposed of—perhaps back to the hotel. While this is happening, Ananias is sent by Christ from the Heaven-pageant to baptize him. With this achieved, the Heaven-pageant moves away to the vacant side of the square, and Saul retires to the hotel to change his costume. Speeches by the Poet, punctuated by a dance, provide continuity until the Knights come into the center of the *platea* and report their news to Caiaphas and Annas in the Jerusalem-cart. The machinists in the Heaven-pageant now intervene with thunder and lightning to introduce the diablerie (who carry a chair for Belial) and again to cover their exit. Saul then returns to the *platea* in his disciple's clothes to preach his sermon. The servant of the Jerusalem-cart (who was formerly in attendance on Saul) now acts as an intermediary between Caiaphas in Jerusalem and Saul in Damascus. Saul then retires (*recedit paulisper*) while Caiaphas and Annas consult between themselves and instruct their servant to return to Damascus and imprison Saul. The Angel then intervenes from the Heaven-pageant to warn Saul what is afoot. The Poet provides the Epilogue and all the actors together with both wagons depart, singing the Latin hymn as they go. The whole play is over and done with inside an hour or at most an hour and a half.

Very different is the other Digby play, *Mary Magdalene*. This is not only a much longer play, but scenically much more demanding, and spectacular. It is constructed in three distinct sections, although divided technically within the text into two parts. The action in part I involves twenty changes of locality and ranges over nine separate localities: part II specifies at least fifteen separate localities and thirty-two shifts of locality. There is a *platea*, but, with the exception of Hell, no scaffolds or stages, and no stage-directions instructing characters to move *down* into the place or *up* onto scaffolds. Angels descend from heaven and Mary herself is received into heaven; but that's not quite the same thing.

In this respect the play differs sharply from *St. Meriasek*, where all the principal characters are presented on their scaffolds and descend into the *platea* before they can participate in the action. The script of *St. Meriasek* is carefully orchestrated to facilitate staging on and within an earthwork "round" (so is the script of *"The Castle of Perseverance"*). The text of the play of *Mary Magdalene* just as certainly is not. This is not to say that it could not be performed "in the round"; I fancy it could. Yet it does suggest that the author had some other form of staging in mind. One clue as to what this might have been is provided by a peculiar feature of the text itself: the survival in thinly disguised shapes of several cyclic plays. The most obvious of these are the *Visitatio Sepulchri* of scene 25 and the *Assumption of the Virgin* of scene 47. Scarcely less obvious are the origins of scenes 4 and 15 in the plays of *Herod the Great* and the *Harrowing of Hell*. The presence of Pontius Pilate in the play (scenes 5 and 28) and of the two scenes covering the death and resurrection of Lazarus (18 and 20) is equally suspicious. And do the several scenes on board ship indicate the adaptation and inclusion of Noah's Ark? In short, there is a good case for suggesting that the *fons et origo* of this play was not dramatic treatment of a legendary narrative of Mary Magdalene's life *per se*, but theatrical adaptation of an extensive stock of existing scenic units to a new purpose. In other words, for some local reason—perhaps novelty, perhaps a patronal festival, perhaps a ban on the local Corpus Christi Cycle—a new play was devised by adapting legendary material relating to Mary Magdalene's life to conform with the stock of scenic costumes and properties already possessed by the players. If this were so, then comparison with the York and Beverley *Pater Noster* Plays, the Lincoln play of *Tobias* and even the Coventry play of *The Destruction of Jerusalem* would at once become legitimate.

I cannot provide in the space available to me a scene-by-scene description of how I think this play was staged: that warrants a whole paper to itself. I can however postulate that *Ludus Coventriae*, with its simultaneous staging in and around a single acting area, provides the best English duplicate of the likely production conventions, and that *Le Mystère des Trois Doms* amplifies this picture, if French example can be admitted (see fig. 3). Furthermore, if

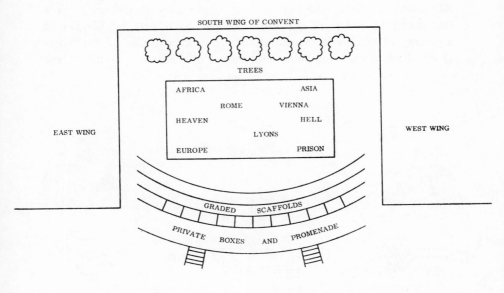

Fig. 3. A reconstructed ground plan of the layout of the town square for a performance of *Le Mystère des Trois*, Romans, 1509.

an East Anglian provenance can be agreed upon, and a date of composition as late as the 1520's can be allowed, I would surmise the genesis of this play to lie in an attempt to salvage something from a decision to drop the Corpus Christi Cycle in that community. Ipswich might be a likely candidate, since the Corpus Christi Cycle there was laid aside as early as 1511 in favor of a play about St. George and was only revived once in the six years between 1513 and 1519. The situation in Ipswich is admittedly unusual, but it

warns us against wholly uncritical acceptance of Father Gardiner's
proposition in *Mysteries' End* that the *only* reason for the disappear-
ance of the cycles from English theatrical life was the Reformation.
Whether performed at Ipswich, however, or elsewhere, my own
preference of venue for the actual staging of the Digby *Mary
Magdalene* is a field, like that at Bassingbourne with its barn, where
use could be made of the local terrain, as it was by Sir David
Lyndsay at Cupar in Scotland for the performance of *Ane Satyre
of the Thrie Estaitis* on Whit-Tuesday, 1552. There, (see fig. 4) the

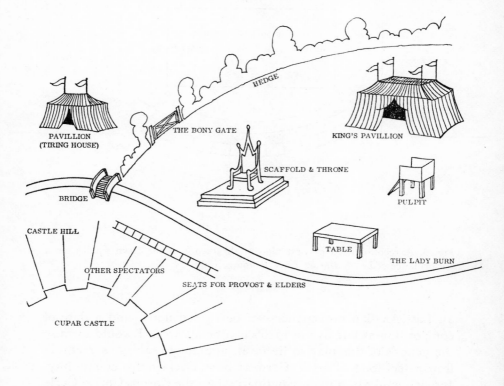

Fig. 4. A reconstructed ground plan of the stage and the auditorium for a performance of Sir David Lindsay's *Ane Satyre of the Three Estaitis*, Cupar, Fife,
Scotland, on Whit-Tuesday, 1552.

gate and the bridge of the text and stage directions corresponded to the actual Bonygate and the actual Ladyburn stream of the terrain chosen for the *platea*.[8] Given a field of this sort, with a stream and a small island as integral elements of the *platea*, it would be easy to understand why no less than six scenes of part II of the *Mary Magdalene* play are ship scenes—one fifth, that is, of the whole play. (Ipswich, incidentally, was especially proud of its ship-pageant).

IV

It is time now to bring this essay to a close, and I would like to do so with some observations arising directly from an actual revival of a Saint Play, *St. Meriasek*. On this I can speak with some authority, as I not only directed it but, owing to the untimely illness of the actor in the title role, had to play the part of the Saint myself for two nights! First, then, I must observe that, having decided to present it in early of March 1969 because we were already committed to reviving the Cornish Cycle in St. Piran's Round in July, we had no choice but to present it indoors. This meant cutting the central sections of the play dealing with the conversion of the Emperor Constantine, partly because we could not meet the casting requirements, and partly because we could not get the forest fire that destroys the outlaws passed by the Fire Authorities! Thus, confronted with a shortened text of no particular literary merit which relied for its impact almost wholly upon simple narrative and theatricality, I felt obliged to give free rein in my imagination to Professor Kolve's remarks about "game" and "play" in medieval drama and to Dr. Weiner's observations about the unmotivated representation of character and event in medieval acting.[10] With this assistance I came to realize that the sequences of short or very short scenes, the frequent changes of locality, the miracles—in short, all those problems of the script which in any realistic, pictorial concept of the play are virtually insoluble, short of recourse to *Quo Vadis* motion-picture treatment—all of these problems could be reduced to manageable proportions *provided* the make-believe element in production were exploited rather than suppressed. To this end the banquet of scene 5 was presented by means of a flat table out of which all the glasses, decanters, and dessert dishes stood up at the pull of a single-string. The Saint was conveyed from Brittany to Cornwall and back again by means of a toy ship operated on the push-me-pull-you principle, with other actors to assist choreographically as wind and waves (see plate 1). By such means, all the scenic problems of the play became sources of fun and delight to both spectators and actors: but, in resolving this problem, this device created another and more serious one for the actors themselves—how to combine this fluency of narrative with any degree of conviction in the action.

For actors and audiences of the Middle Ages, no problem of this sort would have arisen: to them saints, along with personalities of Biblical history, were far less distinctly defined as historical characters than they are to audiences for whom personal and daily access to the Bible was to become the norm rather than the exception. At the same time, the saints and martyrs, while entirely familiar in the pictured forms of stained glass, fresco and statuary, were elevated in medieval minds above and beyond normal human beings by the remoteness of their achievements: what they had accomplished in the name of their faith set them apart from common men of whatever degree. As with all heroes, the more local the saint, the keener the partisan interest in his life and works. Even God, in these terms of reference, could readily be presented on the stage as a combination of *rex* and *paterfamilias* without risk of blasphemy or disrespect, even in Protestant consciences (see plate 2).

The solution adopted to this problem in rehearsal was to abstract from the text the bare bones of the emotional conflict or mood of each scene, and then to improvise in modern terms of reference a scene with characters of similar social status and with a similar beginning, climax and resolution. This we worked up to a pitch where the actors could shout at each other, cry, and laugh because of the situations that arose naturally out of their improvised relationships. We then reverted to the actual text and endeavored to

Photograph by Roger Gilmour

Plate 1. St. Meriasek being conveyed from Brittany to Cornwall.

Photograph by Roger Gilmour

Plate 2. Portrayal of God as a combination of *rex* and *paterfamilias* in John Bale's *God's Promises*, 1969, Drama Department, University of Bristol.

Photograph by Roger Gilmour

Plate 3. This photograph was taken during rehearsal when the entire Cornish mystery cycle was revived by the Drama Department, University of Bristol, at St. Pirans Round, Cornwall, during the summer of 1969.

impose the emotional patterns discovered within the improvisations upon the course of the scripted narrative. Thus, while this technique was imposed uniformly upon the script, all changes of setting, lighting and costume were effected frankly but discreetly in full view of the audience, as has subsequently been done by Peter Brook in his highly-praised production of *A Midsummer Night's Dream*. Having committed ourselves to this convention, we took it as far as we could go. (In the event, some of these changes were not as discreet as I could have wished, owing to a failure on the part of some actors to recognize how conspicuous any unrehearsed actions "off-stage" might appear) .

Our starting point was a multilevel *platea* and a troupe of players equipped with a stock of costumes and scenic emblems. The troupe was one of "hippies" who introduced themselves and their equipment to the strains of the Beatles' "All You Need Is Love." This seemed to imprint the anti-materialist and anti-establishment quality of the Saint's character and actions as firmly and effectively upon the audience's imagination as could be managed in a wholly unsectarian way. Obviously, I cannot say whether this approach proved acceptable and convincing to every spectator, but it was at least successful in provoking laughter where this was allowable and of eliminating it altogether in those sequences which were designed by the author to be taken seriously. Many claimed to have been moved by the Saint's death, and this could not have happened had the audience not been brought to meet him and the personal qualities he represented.

A great act of faith on the part of all concerned was required to enter upon this experiment; but it was rewarded by a vision, however dimly grasped, of the degree of artistic skill and assurance which our forefathers possessed when they came to devise these Saint Plays. For, not only had they mastered the delicate art of instructing by entertaining, but they had discovered conventions of stage-craft through which to reduce the requirements of a narrative that ranged the frontiers of the known world to dimensions that could readily be provided by their fellow men in market-place, church, field or arena. In the realm of drama this is no less of an achievement, I would submit, than the construction of a cathedral in that of architecture. In more recent terms, it proved an indispensable prelude to the revival of the whole Cornish Mystery Cycle in St. Pirans "Round" that same summer (see plate 3).[11]

NOTES

1. O.B. Hardison, Jr., *Christian Rite and Christian Drama in the Middle Ages* (Baltimore, 1965).

2. Carleton Brown, "An Early Mention of a St. Nicholas Play in England," *Studies in Philology*, 38 (1931), 594–601,

3. Otto Pacht, *The Rise of Pictorial Narrative in Twelfth-Century England* (Oxford, 1962).

4. A. Harbage and S. Schoenbaum, *Annals of English Drama, 975-1700* (London, 1964).

5. "Lundonia pro spectaculis theatralibus, pro ludis scenicis, ludos habet sanctiores, repraesentationes miraculorum quae sancti confessores operati sunt, sive repraesentationes spassionum quibus clavint constantia maityrum." (E. K. Chambers, *The Mediaeval Stage*, 2 vols. [London, 1903], II, 379–80.) See also A.W. Pollard, *English Miracle Plays, Moralities and Interludes*, revised ed. (Oxford, 1965), p. xix. I am grateful to my colleague Dr. Neville Denny for drawing my attention to this important reference.

6. B. Ten Brink, *History of English Literature*, W.C. Robinson trans., 3 vols. (London, 1893), p. 239. See also Murray Roston, *Biblical Drama in England* (Evanston, 1968), pp. 20–32.

7. Glynne Wickham, *Early English Stages*, 2 vols. (London, 1958–63), II, 62–63.

8. John MacQueen, "Ane Satyre of the Thrie Estaitis," *Studies in Scottish Literature*, 3 (January, 1966), 139–43.

9. V.A. Kolve, *The Play Called Corpus Christi* (Stanford, 1966).

10. A.B. Weiner, *Mézières' Fourteenth Century Prompt Book* (New Haven, 1958).

11. Since handing over the typescript of this essay, I have encountered two further references to Saint Plays in England which are sufficiently relevant to matters discussed in this paper to warrant inclusion in the only manner now possible, an extended footnote.

The first of these references concerns the play of St. Mary Magdalene in the Digby MS in the Bodleian Library. It is an entry in the *Liber Computi* of Magdalen College, Oxford; dated 1506 to 1507, it reads,

Solutum domino burges pro scriptura lusi b(ea)te marie magdalene...x[P]
Solutum Kendall pro diligentia sua in luso Sancte marie Magdalene
Mandato vice presidentis...xij[d]

Sir Edmund Chambers, making use of J.R. Bloxam and W.D. Macray, *A Register of the Members of St. Mary Magdalen College, Oxford*, (Oxford, 1894–1911), calls attention to this entry and adds that Burgess was paid a further five shillings "for some music" while an Edward Martyn, M.A., provided some songs. (*Mediaeval Stage*, II, 248).

It would be rash to regard the text of the Digby MS as being associated with this Oxford play; but the correspondence between the date of the Oxford play and the writing of the Digby play is interesting, as is the patronal motivation for the writing of the Oxford play. (See Malone Society, *Collections V*, [1959–60], p. 46.)

The second reference comes from Shrewsbury. The Bailiffs who kept the Corporation Accounts record two items in 1516 relating to a Saint Play in the town.

In vino, pomis, waffers, at aliis novellis datis et expenditis super abbatem Salop et famulos suos ad ludum et demonstrationem martirorum Felicianae et Sabinae in quarera post muros.

In regardo dato lusoris eiusdem martirii tunc temporis hoc anno.

This is another instance of a Saint Play being performed in a large open-air environment, the quarry. Bounded by the river Severn and the hill on which the town stands, this old quarry was frequently used for performances of plays. Traces of a seated amphitheatre are said to have been visible there late in the eighteenth century. (See H. Owen and J.B. Blakeway, *History of Shrewsbury*, (1889 or 1825) vol. 1, pp. 262–328, and Chambers, *Mediaeval Stage*, II, pp. 251 and 394–95).

This setting, as can be seen even now that much of the area is blocked by buildings, has obvious affinities with the site at Cupar for the performance of *Ane Satyre of the Thrie Estaitis* and with the demands of the stage directions in the Digby Play of St. Mary Magdalene.

THE ORIGINS OF THE *QUEM QUAERITIS* AND THE EASTER SEPULCHRE MUSIC-DRAMA, AS DEMONSTRATED BY THEIR MUSICAL SETTINGS

William L. Smoldon

I AM PROPOSING in this essay to deal with a matter which seems once more to have come into controversy—the origins of the *Quem quaeritis* dialogue. On the one hand, there is the feeling that Karl Young and his followers have said the last word on the subject; on the other, there appears to be an opinion that certain newer *textual* theories fit the *textual* facts better. I believe that I also may have something fresh to say. But my approaches will be on different lines from those that have been followed heretofore.

The "origins" mentioned are of course concerned with the rise of the so-called liturgical dramas of the medieval Church. More than a hundred years have passed since literary scholars began to concern themselves with these phenomena—dramatic activities closely linked with actual medieval Church services. There have been generations of books written on the subject, the most outstanding contribution, perhaps, coming from Karl Young in 1933 (*The Drama of the Medieval Church*).[1] I need not say much concerning his two volumes, since everyone who has wanted to write on the subject for the last few decades has turned to him in order to make use of those dramatic texts that he had with such thoroughness collected, transcribed, and commented upon.

But what has amazed me for many years is the curious blindness that with a few exceptions (e.g., the efforts of Oskar Schönemann and Ferdinando Liuzzi)[2] has possessed a hundred years of scholarship in one essential aspect. When I seek to express what I mean, I am reminded of the occasion, over two and a half years ago, of my addressing the Conference on Medieval Studies at Binghamton. I was then able to project on a screen half-a-dozen reproductions of manuscript pages ranging from the tenth century to the fifteenth which showed examples of that *Quem quaeritis* dialogue that in due course became the core of the *Visitatio Sepulchri* music-drama. I pointed out that every one of the texts shown had its concomitant music written above the syllables. It was clear from the photographs that the notational styles employed varied enormously from version to version, from signs that looked more like shorthand than anything else, to square notes accurately placed on four-line staves.[3] I also mentioned at the time that these photographs were but part of a collection of several hundred concerned with Church music-drama which I happened to possess. A matter always to be borne in mind is that every syllable of the uttered texts of these compositions, whether trope or drama, was *sung*, and that if a manuscript turned up with music absent from the familiar text it was because we had here an *ordinarium* or some similar service-book, which for the time being was concentrating on rubrics rather than on the materials of performance. Another matter to which I gave emphasis was that, however different the notations that set the three *Quem quaeritis* sentence exchanges in the different photographic examples, the musical settings could always be recognized as having sprung from some common prototype, whatever small variations may be found to have occurred locally in various parts of Christendom through the centuries.

The plain fact is that for far too long writers on the subject have chosen to disregard half the evidence that the original documents have to show, with, as I shall later demonstrate, quite a number of regrettable results, Karl Young being an offender among the rest. He mentioned in his preface that he didn't feel called on to apologize for not considering the musical settings—which was a pity, since it caused too many lesser lights to follow his example. As early as 1860 the famous musicologist and literary scholar Edouard de Coussemaker published some transcriptions (texts and music) of certain of these drama manuscripts that had recorded their settings on stave lines. The book was *Drames liturgiques du moyen âge*, and in his introduction he was somewhat ironic towards his fellow scholars and editors, as the following passages, given in translation, illustrate:

...but their publications [those of his fellow editors] which reproduce the dramatic pieces are incomplete: there is a regrettable omission. The editors have despoiled them of the music which accompanied them, and which is an integral and substantial part of them....What would one think of a writer who, wishing to initiate us into the operas that were played before (for example) Louis XIV, would be contented to reproduce the libretti of Quinault?[4]

(Philippe Quinault was, of course, the poet dedicated all his life to the famous composer, Jean Baptiste Lully.) Coussemaker's irony remains much to the point at the present day. The libretti of these *music*-dramas are still studied to the exclusion of the *music*. Few writers, it would seem, have realized that they are dealing not with dramas, but music-dramas, or, in other words, *operas*. My views are based on a general grasp of the music of the whole range of the Church music-dramas through the centuries, since I have transcribed almost all of them from photos of the original manuscripts or the manuscripts themselves; and, through public performances of some of them *as* music-dramas, have, I hope, shown these to be living works of art. I think, however, that before continuing with my subject I had better justify my claims in regard to the possession of musical evidence. These are based on the acquisition and close study of a considerable collection of photos of manuscripts, already mentioned, which, I believe, include all surviving examples that are worthwhile considering. They are my private property and represent years of such collecting.

In the early 1930s I was already a professional musician with a University degree. I then became a student of English literature at King's College, London, under the aegis of Dr. A. W. Reed, Professor of English at the University of London. When it came to the beginnings of medieval drama, I learned with interest that the

Quem quaeritis trope was not merely spoken, but (so I was told) "chanted." When, after the lecture, I asked the Professor if he could tell me what the music was to which the dialogue was sung, he replied that he hadn't the faintest idea. But after a pause and a penetrating look, he added, "It might be a good move if *you* tried to find out." That I proceeded to do, but it took quite a time.

Until the outbreak of the war with Hitler, I corresponded and travelled in Europe gathering manuscript photos and copies of those tropes and acted versions that showed their musical settings. The gathering was a slow process, but by 1939 I had transcribed enough material together with its music to permit the Plainsong and Medieval Music Society to stage *sung* performances of several Easter *Visitatio Sepulchri* versions at King's Weigh House Chapel, London, in March 1939; an event that I should like to put on record here. Previously, in 1933, I had met with Karl Young's newly published volumes, which were very useful to me in my search for original manuscripts. I had the pleasure of personal contact and friendship with Karl Young, and we corresponded right up to the year of his untimely death.

One of my tasks was to make practical modern readings of the notations of various types which I had tracked down. This I did by following (at, of course, a lower level) the techniques of the Benedictines of Solesmes who, through long years of photographing, charting, and studying manuscript service books belonging to all significant centuries, had been able to recover the authentic Gregorian music of the Roman Church.

In my lesser way I made comparative charts of the *Quem quaeritis* dialogue music as found in various countries of Christendom and as traced through the centuries. I made a separation between French and French-influenced versions as against those that were German and German influenced, with separate consideration for Italian and Spanish manuscripts. Also, I isolated all those sentences with all their musical settings that are to be found linked with the *Quem quaeritis* dialogue in both its trope form and in the dramatic expansions of the *Visitatio Sepulchri* type— whether these additions were other tropes, liturgical borrowings (antiphons and the like), or specially composed items, prose or verse. I took due note as to which particular *Quem quaeritis* versions (trope or dramatic) these additional compositions were to be found attached, and, when it proved necessary, made comparative charts of their settings. Such resources of musical information sometimes served to identify a sentence when no more than an ambiguous *incipit* happened to be given in the original manuscript. Regarding the material of these charts: in earlier manuscripts the music is to be found in a cryptic notation called "neumes." These served not to give the exact details of a melody, but merely to *remind* a singer (or more probably a cantor) of a tune that he had previously learned by heart. The various neume shapes distinguished the number of notes that were to be allotted to each Latin syllable; this without giving their exact pitches. Only gradually came precision, first by more exact "heighting" round a single horizontal line (which in due course was given a clef sign), and then by the ultimate development to the four-line stave.[5]

I will now give some practical illustrations of the power of music to solve problems that seem to have baffled "textual" writers. Plate 1 is a reproduction of a page from a Gradual of the late twelfth century.

The musical setting above the text consists of unheighted St. Gall neumes. At the top of the page the last responsory of Easter Matins is ending, to the usual service chant-music. It is succeeded by a choral piece, which introduces the little drama and no doubt covered the movements of the Marys to the Sepulchre. It is an invented composition, poetic text and music unique to the Bamberg center through the centuries. Karl Young prints the five lines (1, p. 585), which begin, *"Ad tumulum venere gementes..."* ("They come to the sepulchre lamenting..."). He points out, as the photograph shows, that each line of the text is followed by a letter A..., with a welter of close-packed neumes overhead. He speculates on these last, wondering whether they represent some kind of *jubilus,* or an *Alleluia* setting. They are in fact neither. I was able to work out their solution from a later and staved Bamberg manuscript. It then becomes apparent that here is an early and charming example of the "echo" technique, a liturgical trick found more readily in later centuries, whereby one side of a choir sang a phrase, the melody of which was vocalized to a vowel sound by the other. Figure 1 shows the first line of a modern transcription, the music rendered in the first rhythmic mode.

Ad _ tu-mu-lum ve-ne-re ge-men- tes, A ———

("*They come un-to the se-pul-chre mourn-ing*")

Fig. 1. A modern transcription of the first line of the manuscript page reproduced in Plate 1.

A knowledge of medieval Gregorian music would have shown that the "Alleluia" speculation was also a barren one. The word having four syllables, whatever neume-music was set to it would be written as four separate entities. In the manuscript photo, the lines towards the bottom of the page show a number of "alleluia" examples, the word being abbreviated to "*a e u ia.*"

As another example of musical detective work I will quote the case of the thirteenth century Zurich, Zentralbibl., Rheinau XVIII manuscript (pp. 282-83), a *Visitatio* of some merit. In his commentary upon it Karl Young writes (p. 389): "One is surprised to observe in so careful a composition the incongruity...between the mention of *two* Marys in the introductory antiphon and the actual appearance of *three* upon the stage." The fact is that he looked at the *incipit* of the "antiphon" as given in the manuscript, which consisted of no more than the two words, "*Maria Magdalena...*," and took them to indicate the presence of the official responsory, "*Maria Magdalena et alia Maria ferebant diluculo aromata....*" Strangely enough, he already knew that there were *four* compositions in use at the time which began with "*Maria Magdalena...*," and, moreover, he printed all four texts on page 601 of his first volume. The fourth of them, an "invented" composition, begins, "*Maria Magdalene et Maria Jacobi et Salome sabbato quidem....*" I have the musical settings of all four of them, in both neume and fixed note form, and when I compare these with the Rheinau manuscript *incipit*, I find that the Rheinau neumes indicate that the setting was most likely that of the *fourth* text, which did indeed mention *three* Marys.[6] So probably the Rheinau playwright is owed an apology. Karl Young observes that "when only the *incipit* of an 'antiphon' is given, it will hardly be possible to identify it exactly." In that he was mistaken.

My regard for the tremendous achievements of Karl Young and my reverence for him as a great scholar leave me a little uncomfortable when I carp at his minor lapses. Thus I welcome the chance of springing to his defense when he is unjustly accused. A fairly recent publication, *Christian Rite and Christian Drama in the Middle Ages*, by Professor O.B. Hardison, has much to say regarding the origins of the *Quem quaeritis* trope and the *Visitatio Sepulchri*, and does so, much to my amazement, without any reference to their musical settings, or indeed to the Gregorian music of the Roman liturgy, the ceremonies of which play such a part in the author's arguments.[7] However, this is a matter for later consideration. For the moment I will concentrate on a rebuke that he offers to Karl Young. The latter, in the course of commenting on the texts of certain *Quem quaeritis* trope versions, had concluded that in a number of cases the word "Resurrexi*t*" was a scribal error for "Resurrexi," the first word of the Introit of the Easter Mass, which the *Quem quaeritis* trope was introducing in the normal way. Hardison remains unconvinced. Leaning heavily as he does on the Karl Young volumes as his source of quotations of dramatic texts, he names in a footnote the pages on which there occur *Quem quaeritis* dialogue versions where the "Resurrexit" *incipit* appears to him to be ambiguous. He cites five versions in all, and writes:

... tenth and eleventh century versions regularly end with the antiphons *Resurrexit Dominus* and *Surrexit Dominus* even when they are part of Matins rather than Mass. It is therefore not at all clear that *Resurrexit* is a simple scribal error. It could equally be a transcription of an antiphon *incipit* from a version associated with Easter Mass.[8]

It could be nothing of the sort! I turn now, not to secondhand texts, but to photos of each of the manuscripts themselves that

Hardison indicates. If he had worked from the originals instead of from Karl Young's "libretti," and if he had known anything at all about Gregorian music as applied to the liturgy he would have seen staring at him above the numerous incorrect *Resurrexit* versions in question the age-old neumes of the opening music of the Introit of the Easter Mass: *Resurrexi, et adhuc tecum sum...* Here (fig. 2) are the neumes of *Resurrexi*, the word normally found standing alone as the *incipit* which indicates the advent of the **Easter Introit**.

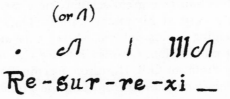

Fig. 2. The medieval neumes of *Resurrexi*, the first word of the Introit of the Easter Mass; an *incipit* which is usually found rounding off the *Quem quaeritis* dialogue in its trope form.

In a modern service book the neumes will be found transcribed as in figure 3:

Fig. 3. A transcription of the medieval neumes of *Resurrexi*...into Gregorian plainchant notation, as found in a modern service book.

In the tenth and eleventh centuries the second neume is sometimes found as a *clivis* (F, D) instead of a *torculus* (D, F, D), but always there stands out the *tristropha* of the last syllable.

Let us now look at a reproduction of one of the versions mentioned by Hardison, who quotes it as coming from Young 1, page 206. The manuscript is Modena, MS 0. 1. 7 (plate 2).

The photograph shows the dialogue music, leading to an extra trope (*Alleluia, resurrexit Dominus hodie...*) and after that to the first word of the Introit with its correct music. But the scribe, influenced probably by what he has just set down, writes incorrectly, under the Introit music, *Resurrexit*. Then comes the rubric *Al* (i.e., *Aliter*, "otherwise"). An alternative final trope has been provided, and this one again leads to the Introit, with its music. This time we have the correct *Resurrexi*, fitted to the same official setting, followed by the rest of the Introit written out in full with its music. Karl Young's correction was needed.

I cannot afford to give any more illustrations, but I have the photos of all the manuscript pages concerned in my possession. In Hardison's next example (Rome, Bibl. Vatic. MS lat. 4770, fol. 117r., a tenth to eleventh century missal)—I am handicapped by the fact that the musical settings are omitted, but when there twice occurs the sentence *Resurrexit et adhuc tecum sum...*, can we doubt the correctness of Young's omission of the *t*? Even when one "*Resurrexit*" stands by itself, it clearly marks the beginning of another repetition of the Introit.

Hardison next quotes B.N. MS lat. 1119, from St. Martial de Limoges. There can be no manner of doubt that "*Resur...*" represents *Resurrexi*, as Karl Young assumes, since the first two Introit neumes are given, correctly, above the syllables. As a preliminary to the next (internal) troping of the Introit, *Resurrexi* is written out in full, and correctly, with the correct neumes above. On my own account I have surveyed the rest of that end-of-century Limoges group, concerning *Resurrexi*, and found a mixed state of responsibility. More often than not we have the full opening sentence, latinity and neumes all correct; some *Resurrexi* instances without any neumes; a few unashamed *Resurrexit et adhuc tecum sum*, but with occasionally a cancelling *punctum* under the *t*, to show that the error had been spotted even before the advent of Karl Young.

Another of Hardison's choices is Apt, MS 4, fol. 33v.-34v. The manuscript, which has clear, unheighted, Catalan-style neumes with some interpolations by an Aquitaine scribe, represents, as far as the *Quem quaeritis* dialogue and the Easter Introit are concerned, a flood—a riot—of further introductory, concluding and intercalatory tropes. The changes rung on *Resurrexit* and *Resurrexi* become almost amusing, but always they are accompanied by the Introit neumes, to make the situation clear. The scribe was twice wrong and twice right, but one of the correct results was obtained by smearing out the errant *t*. Karl Young was right every time.

Hardison's last example, Brescia, MS H. vi. 11, fol. 30, an *ordinarium* of the fifteenth century, is, of course, by its very type and purpose deprived of its music, but surely there is no reason to doubt Karl Young's corrections, seeing that we have once again repetitions of the troped Introit, and remembering the fact that *officium* (as Young points out) implies in France and elsewhere, "Introit," even in the form of *"offitium Resurexit"*! (The latinity of this particular scribe must have been past praying for.)

I have been dealing with these examples to some length, not so much for the purpose of bolstering the case of Karl Young and myself (which is abundantly proved anyway), but mainly to show how limited is the horizon of Professor Hardison when it is essential to the subject that musical evidence must be considered. One last reference to that paragraph of his which I quoted on page 127. If I understand rightly what he means by "regularly," then his first sentence, concerning *Alleluia, resurrexit Dominus*[9] and *Surrexit Dominus*, is not correct, as a close inspection of all the manuscripts concerned should have revealed. Tenth and eleventh century versions of the dialogue, whether trope or *Visitatio*, vary in their choice of concluding sentences, and do *not* tie themselves down to *Alleluia, resurrexit Dominus hodie*...and *Surrexit Dominus de sepulchro*. ... Many prefer *Ad sepulchrum residens* ..., *En ecce completum* ... or *Surrexit enim sicut*.... Incidentally, *Alleluia, resurrexit Dominus hodie,* ... is a trope, not an official antiphon. Also, the two texts which Hardison names have each two different settings, representing each two separate compositions; in the first case marking French and Italian preferences; in the second, the difference between a liturgical setting (as in Hartker's *Antiphonale*) and a "free" one, apparently German in origin.

One other last word, concerning scribal errors. Only a paleographer dealing with the handwritten parchments of the period can have any idea of the rank carelessness and ignorance displayed by *some* scribes. One has to avoid the temptation to regard every puzzle as being the result of a scribal error. Among their number there seem to have been travelling "professionals." It does seem at times as if the latinity of some of them were sadly to seek.[10]

I must turn now to my main task, dealing with the origin of the *Quem quaeritis* dialogue. One would think that it was a straightforward matter to suppose that the *Quem quaeritis* trope, like the hundreds and hundreds of tropes that came into anonymous existence, was *composed* for a single particular purpose, in its own particular case to attach itself to the Easter Introit. As that historian of tropes and sequences, Jacques Handschin, remarks: "*Every trope is in principle intended to combine with a given Gregorian song....*" Yet in the book that I have already mentioned, *Christian Rite and Christian Drama in the Middle Ages*, Professor O. B. Hardison advances the theory that both the Easter trope dialogue and the Easter Sepulchre music-drama have their origins, not as set out by Young and a number of previous literary historians, but from already existing Church ceremonies of a dramatic nature. To quote his own words, "An analysis of *Quem quaeritis* manuscripts in these terms consistently leads to the conclusion that the dialogue originated not as an Easter trope but as a ceremony associated with the vigil Mass" (p. 219).

The "terms" on which he bases his analysis, as one will not now be surprised to discover, include no reference to, nor quotation from the *music* of the Easter *Quem quaeritis* dialogue. He displays deep knowledge as to the ceremonies and practices of the medieval Church; altogether, his claim to speak with some authority on the subject of "Christian Rite" seems substantiated. But in facing up to the histrionic part of his task he betrays himself by his title, for he is dealing not with "Christian Drama" but "Christian *Music-Drama*," and he is therefore, as I have said concerning others, working half-blind. In any case, I should have thought that for a full understanding and appreciation of the ancient ceremonial, one should have a grasp also of the glorious, timeless Gregorian chant which accompanies the service texts, and which stands, as Willi Apel has said, "in the relation of a peer to that liturgy."

Hardison's theory leaves me wondering whether I am supposed to believe that *all* tropes have been derived from previously existing liturgical ceremonies, or whether that origin is peculiar to *"Quem quaeritis in sepulchro ?..."* It appears that Hardison has not been able to discover surviving examples of the ceremony that he presupposes, and can do no more than sketch a textual reconstruction, which he confesses to be both "theoretical" and "extremely tentative." He believes that his "vigil Mass" theory is supported by the existence of a text from Tours, written probably in the fifteenth century, and known only from the fact of its being reproduced by the eighteenth century scholar, Martène, who printed it in his well-known publication.[11] Young, who himself printed it (1, pp. 224-25), assumed it to be just another *Quem quaeritis* dialogue text, with some individual additional sentences, and most scholars, I imagine, would agree with him. The version appears to be of the normal *ordinarium* type, with *incipits*, and temporarily deprived of its music, which prevents me from investigating it further.

At this point, I had better make some mention of what we *mean* by "tropes." They were *inventions*, very late inventions, inventions of both texts and music, and as far as the hierarchy were concerned, not always welcome. As is generally known, the practice began, in the ninth century or earlier, of making unauthorized additions to various parts of the Church liturgy. It was one that grew to very great proportions and caused manuscript collections of them, called "tropers," to be established in every country in Christendom. Karl Young has a useful, but non-musical chapter on tropes and sequences, but, generally speaking, "textual" writers do not seem to have realized the enormous magnitude, exuberance, and vitality of this movement. All over Christendom clerics were busy producing swarms of these original compositions with which to garland the ancient liturgy, a process on which authority was inclined more and more to cast a jaundiced eye. As is well known, in the end the Church, through its Council of Trent, dealt drastically with the problem.

There appear to be three categories of tropes proper (I am here disregarding *sequences*) : (1) the purely *musical* type, taking the form of a vocal flourish, a *melisma* in the style of an improvisation added to the normal item; (2) the purely *textual* type, the addition, alone, of a new text, fitted to the notes of an already existing *melisma* (one of the tricks that Notker of St. Gall got up to); (3) the *musical-textual* type, with which we are most concerned. Here we have both new text and new music—complete originality. This type was most frequently employed for troping Introits and the simpler chants of the Ordinary of the Mass (Gloria, Sanctus and Agnus Dei). They were inventions, but their music usually conformed in some ways to the neumatic style of the liturgical item that they were troping and (N.B.) occasionally even borrowed a short *motif* from it. The Introits were favored targets for such troping; none more frequently chosen, as Apel has pointed out, than *"Puer natus est nobis . . .,"* from the Third Mass of Christmas Day. The troping could be *intercalatory* (phrases inserted between the original liturgical phrases), or *introductory*, the trope coming first and leading, in some relevant and linking fashion, into the beginning of the Introit. It is to this last type that the *Quem quaeritis* trope belongs. We have already noted cases of the trope itself receiving a troping—a further sentence or sentences, before and/or after.

I come now to the melody of the three sections of the *Quem quaeritis* dialogue. I say "melody" in the singular, since the setting given originally to the text by some unknown composer is always recognizable, in whatever century and whatever part of Christendom it is encountered. The same might of course, be said of the *Quem quaeritis* text—in the main constant, but with small differentials from place to place. I find, however, that the *musical* differences to be distinguished are far more illuminating for the establishment (or otherwise) of "relationships," as I shall try to show in due course.[12]

Wherever the composition first arose, it seems to have caught on quite quickly and spread everywhere, very much as did certain other "free inventions" of the period—e.g., the *Hodie cantandus* trope of Tuotilo, and quite a number of other, anonymous tropes; the great Sequences, especially the *Victimae Paschali* of Wipo of Burgundy; and that mysterious "respond," *Media Vita*.

133

When we seek among the earliest *Quem quaeritis* examples that have survived we find two that considerably outdate the others in antiquity. These come, respectively, from the Abbey of St. Martial de Limoges and from the Abbey of St. Gall. The Limoges example dates from c. A.D., 930 and the St. Gall from c. 950. Although the Limoges example is the older, its three sections (question, reply, and further statement) have already been themselves troped by the addition of further invented sentences, found both before and after the dialogue. The St. Gall version contains no more than the three sections, the final words *"de sepulchro"* not being found in the Limoges version. The musical settings are manifestly very closely similar, but the small differences between them can be shown to be respectively characteristic of each center and its dependents.

Plates 3 and 4 are photographs of the relative single pages from the two manuscripts mentioned above.

I consider first B.N. 1240, fol. 30v., from St. Martial de Limoges, the Abbey that was a hive of troper activity during the tenth and eleventh centuries. A recent study by the French musicologist Jacques Chailley, *L'Ecole Musicale de St. Martial de Limoges*[13], reveals as never before the monastery's *avant garde* position in the field of musical invention during those centuries, being concerned not only with melody but with the beginnings of polyphony.

MS 1240, f. 30v., a very carelessly written page, shows an early stage of Aquitaine neume notation.[14] The "heightings" of the neumes appear to have been conditioned by the amount of space available between the lines of the text. The dialogue is followed by the familiar French version of *"Alleluia, resurrexit Dominus hodie...,"* and then comes the Easter Introit, troped internally. The "Resurrexi..." *incipit* has got left out (in the case of this scribe one is not surprised), but the *incipits* of *"Posuisti super me ..."* and *"Mirabilis facta est..."* indicate what is going on. Moreover, splashed across the two columns at the top of the page, and imperilling the main text in places, is something that we are getting accustomed to seeing, an alternative troping of the Easter Introit, this time with the *incipits Posuisti...*, *Mirabilis ...* and *Scientia ...* given their usual neumes, both for themselves and their respective *alleluias*.

134

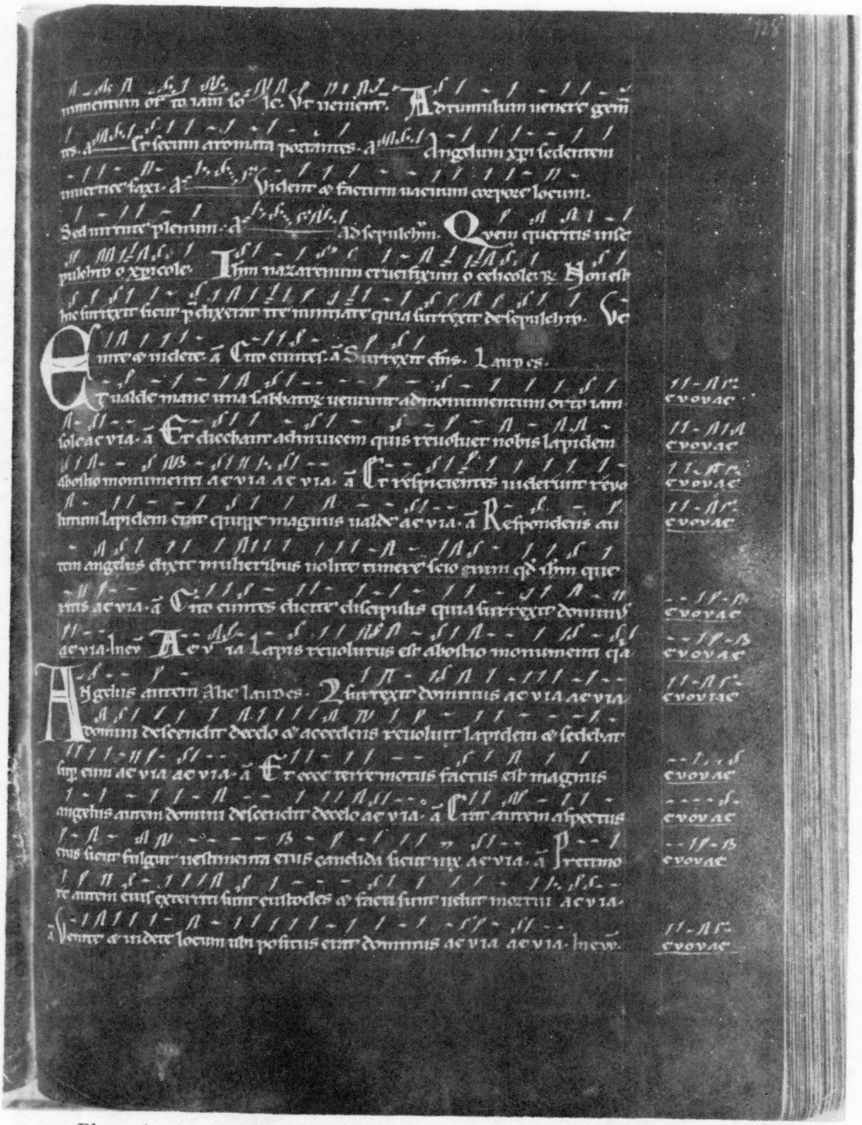

Plate 1. A reproduction from a Gradual of the late twelfth century.

Bamberg, Staatsbibl. MS 22 (Ed. 111.2), fol. 128r.

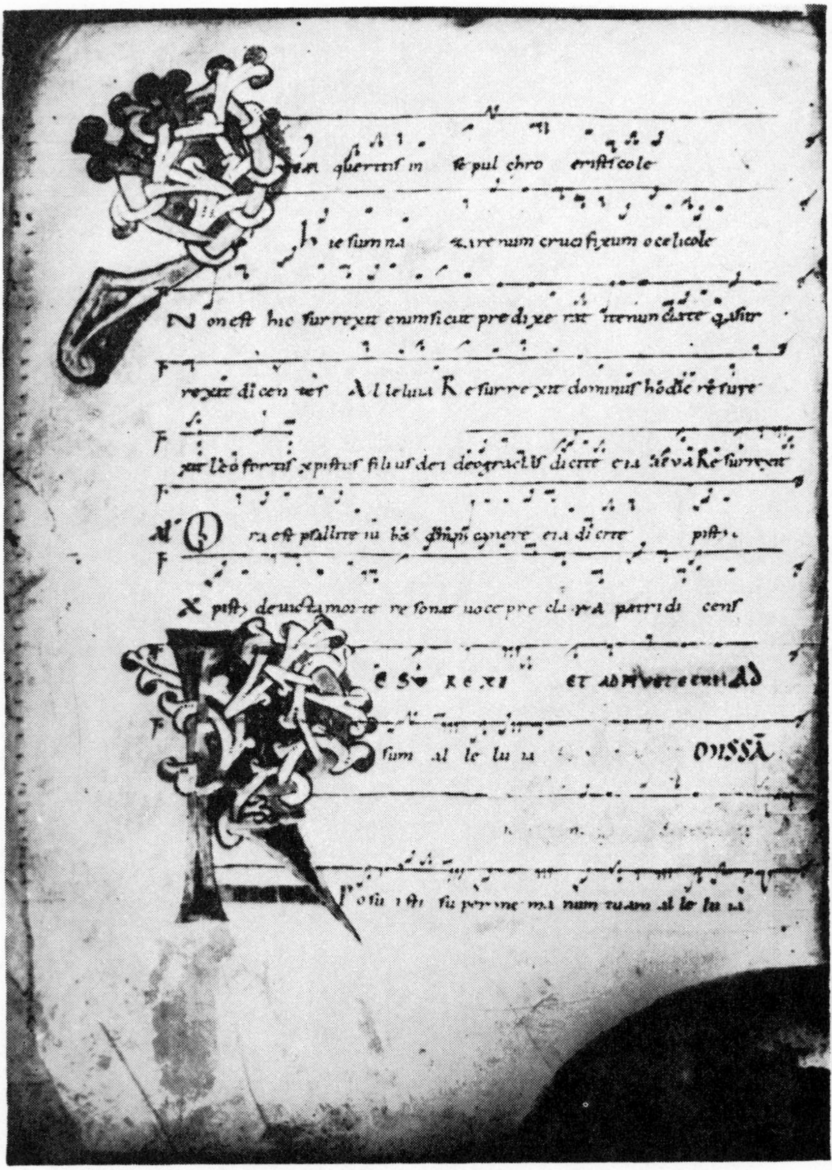

Plate 2. A reproduction of a version of the *Quem quaeritis* dialogue
mentioned by Hardison.

Modena, Bibl. Capit. MS 0.1.7, fol. 102v. (eleventh to twelfth centuries)

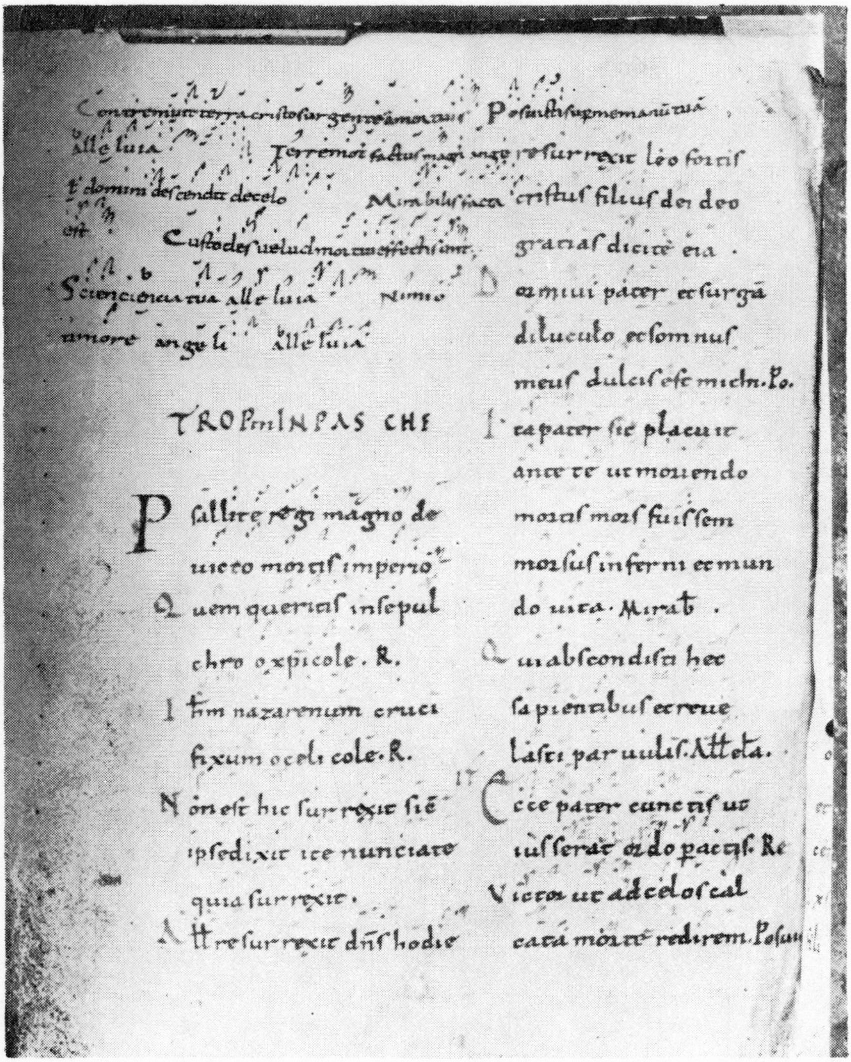

Plate 3. An example of the *Quem quaeritis* trope from the Abbey of St. Martial de Limoges.

Paris, Bibl. Nat. MS lat. 1240, fol. 30v.

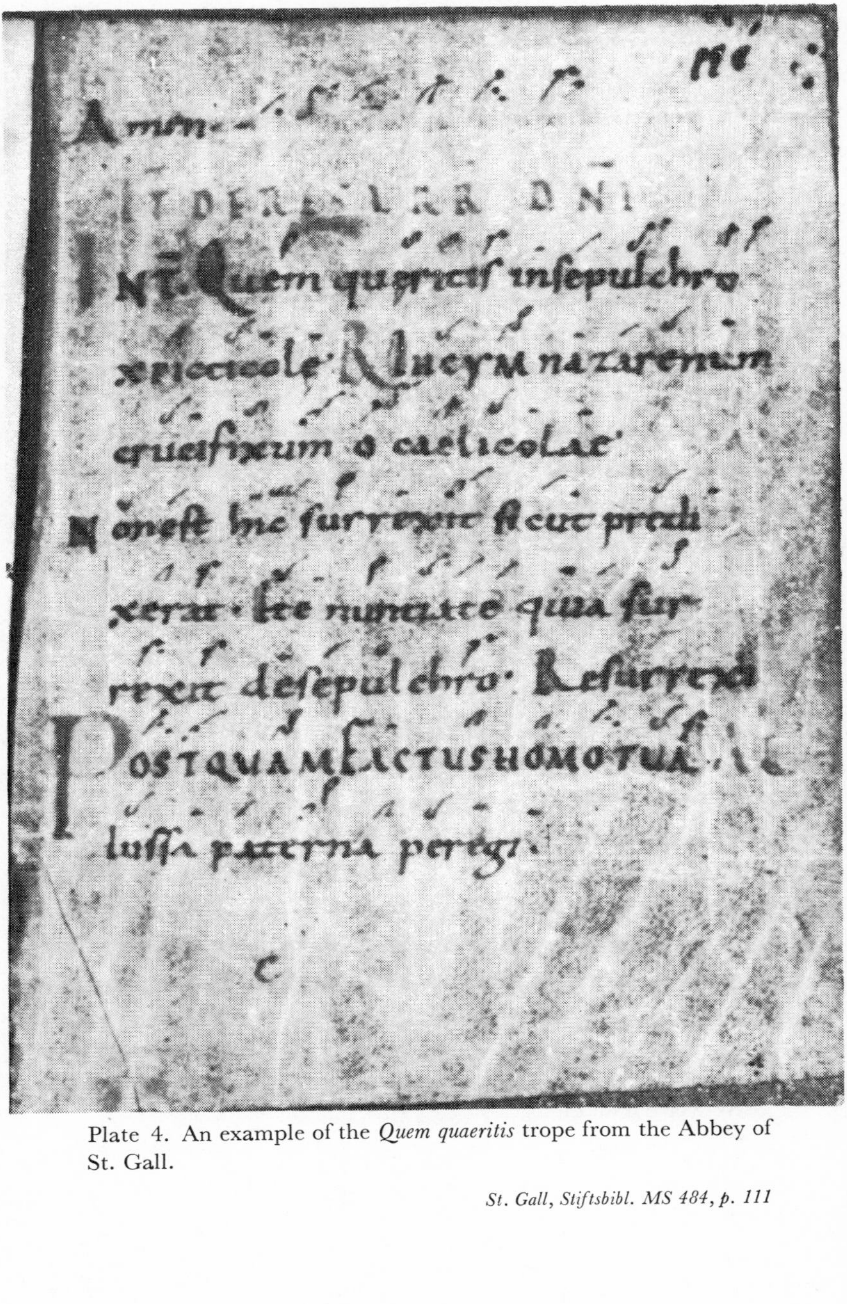

Plate 4. An example of the *Quem quaeritis* trope from the Abbey of St. Gall.

St. Gall, Stiftsbibl. MS 484, p. 111

The *Resurrexi* which began the trope is on the previous page. Pitch-transcription of the dialogue music would have been difficult but for the survival of a group of later Limoges tropers (from the end of the century onward for some decades) showing more clearly, with a few small variations, the same "house" version. No doubt there were many manuscripts which filled the intervening years, but which have perished, or have had their texts and music scraped away to become "palimpsests," put to other uses in a vellum-hungry world. We may reflect also that there may have been similar tropers *earlier* than B.N. 1240, that likewise are lost to us, and, furthermore, that the whole corpus of surviving Church music-drama manuscripts may well represent but a small proportion of what were once in existence.

I give below in modern "free rhythm" notation what I believe to be a reasonably correct version of the Limoges dialogue. As I have remarked, one is frequently uncertain as to the exact height-ing of B.N. 1240's neumes, and certainly there is no Limoges "line" version anywhere near the period, to assist us. I have studied ad-joining pages of B.N. 1240, 30v. These contain some actual litur-gical passages, and from them, their standard settings being known, one can perceive the frequent unreliability of the scribe's heighting. The *Quem quaeritis* musical passage which the tenth and eleventh century groups of Limoges tropers seem to disagree most about is the last, "*Ite, nuntiate quia surrexit,*" where there seem to be two slightly different versions. B.N. 1240's neumes, if one proposes to trust their heighting for this sentence, seem to correspond best with, for example, B.N. 1119, 1120 and that very clearly written B.N. (Nouv. Acq.) MS 1871.

I have transposed the original music up a perfect fourth, with B flat, so that it can be comfortably accommodated on a five-line stave with G clef.

Fig. 4. Limoges' B.N. 1240 is the ealiest surviving example (c. A.D. 930) of the *Quem quaeritis* trope which prefaced the Introit of the Easter Mass. The "heighting" of the Aquitaine neumes must be considered uncertain.

The decipherment of the unheighted neumes of St. Gall 484 was again a matter of appealing to manuscripts of later centuries which showed allegiance to the pioneer manuscript, but which were more definite as to their notes. There is a remarkable "house" conformity among dialogue versions belonging to the St. Gall tradition. Just as the St. Gall style of neume writing is unmistakable, so certain other St. Gall musical "thumb prints" can instantly be recognized. Enough affiliated German versions on stave lines appeared later to

Fig. 5. This is the earliest surviving example (c. A.D. 950) of the *Quem quaeritis* trope belonging to St. Gall and its dependent monasteries. It consists of the three dialogue sentences only, without the additional tropings found in the Limoges version. The neumes are "horizontal," and no reliance can be placed on apparent "heightings." The single note marked with an editorial asterisk is found in later St. Gall versions, sometimes as *sol*, sometimes as *la*. I believe that MS 484 intended *sol*. For an explanation of what seems to be in the transcription an unwarranted vocative "*o*" before "*Christicolae*," see pp. 142–44.

make pretty certain the pitches of the notes of MS 484. They reveal very nearly the same melody as in the Limoges version, but with significant differences. The two main St. Gall "thumb prints" are concerned with (a) the "musical rhyme" at the two vocative phrases, *"Christicolae"* and *"coelicolae,"* and, (b) instances of the German preference in chant-dialect for the frequent substitution of a third for that of a second.

A transcription on a five-line stave, similar to that of B.N. 1240 is set out below. Once again the original is transposed up a fourth.

A few comments on the St. Gall 484 transcription are necessary. (1) This being a St. Gall manuscript, the neumes are sometimes given special shapes and small additions which have certain (perhaps it might be better to say "uncertain") implications as to the duration of the sounds. An example is the "lengthening" sign called *episema*, a short stroke, seen, for example, at the top of the *podatus* belonging to the mid-syllable of the first *"sepulchro,"* and the *clivis* belonging to the last syllable. St. Gall also indulged in the use of certain ("Romanian") letters to indicate variations in the speed of performance, details of expression, and even indications of approximate pitch of the notes. MS 484 happens to be free of these letters, but some problems of interpretation remain.[15] One of them

concerns the *franculus* ſ ʈ —a *virga* followed by an *oriscus* form—

which crops up several times. There seems to be no certainty as to which alternative is right—(a) a *long* single note, or (b) two *short* notes, the second a semitone or tone higher. Later examples of St. Gall *Quem quaeritis* versions seem to give no encouragement for the reading as in (b), but some examples of the neume occurring in St. Gall liturgical manuscripts are officially transcribed in that two-note fashion. The *oriscus* itself, detached, is a controversial neume, a battle-ground for paleographers. In MS 484, at the middle syllable of *"sepulchro,"* it seems to have the function of a liquescent.

The ninth and tenth centuries must have been a busily inventive time for musical clerics endeavouring to put on vellum, in various, regional ways, *representations* of the sounds of the notes of the service settings that had been handed down by memory. They had more courage than Isidore of Seville (early seventh century), whose opinion was that "unless the musical sounds are retained in the human memory, they perish, because they cannot be written down."

(2) The "musical rhyme" between the settings of the two vocative phrases will be evident, even though there appears to be some lengthening of individual notes intended in the *"coelicolae"* phrase. The rhyme could be expressed in terms of sol-fa as rm rd ms r r–. Later dialogue versions from St. Gall used small variations, such as rm rd ms m r–, or rm rd ms mr r–, and/or gave more elaborate settings to the "o" sounds. No doubt I should apologize for introducing sol-fa notation, a form not appreciated by some people, but having the advantage of expressing brief passages of musical sound in the smallest possible space and without calling for bar lines. I have had more to say about it in a note.[16]

(3) Readers who may have consulted Karl Young's photograph of the St. Gall 484 page (op. cit. f. p. 202) will have noticed that I have inserted a vocative "o" (with music) before the word "Christicolae" of my own transcription. I shall offer an explanation of this later.

I should mention at this point that there are two or three French groups of *Quem quaeritis* dialogue versions with their own particular musical rhymes at the vocative phrases (e.g., mr d mfm r–). The individuals of a group show some common features other than the rhyme; in particular, the use of another setting, d r rl, for *"Non est hic."*

(4) As for the German preference in places for the interval of the third instead of the second, this stands out when we compare the respective settings of *"o coelicolae,"* as they occur in B.N. MS 1240 and St. Gall MS 484 respectively – rm rd mḟ m r– as against rm rḋ ms r r–.

Regarding the characteristics of the *Quem quaeritis* melody—with the two early examples of the trope before us, we are as near to the original music as we are ever likely to get. In all its appearances it can be reckoned as a "Dorian" (or "ray") tune; strictly speaking, in Mode II, starting and finishing on D, with its melodic line ranging both above and below that pitch.[17] Before the end of the eleventh century, some versions appeared transposed up a perfect fourth, usually writing in a B flat where needed, but in some cases obviously expecting the singer to supply it with no more than the promptings of *musica ficta*. As for its details: there was always the opening dip, from r to 1, (*"Quem quae—"*). More often than not there is supplied an intermediate, linking light note—a "liquescent" —here concerned with the juxtaposition of those two awkward consonants, "m" and "q." (Sometimes the liquescent is not written in.) With the last syllable of *"quaeritis"* the tune returns to r, usually via two *torculus* forms (1₁dt drd), but these are sometimes simplified to dt₁, dr. The next three notes represent a major characteristic feature, the upward triadic stride, d m s, with the second or third decorated, e.g., d m mfs or dd mfs s (with, of course, other small variations). The setting of the reply, *"Jesum Nazarenum..."* is clearly planned to balance the first phrase, the notes of which, including the upward stride, can be traced in its construction. The setting of *"Non est hic"* is again a characteristic feature. Almost all surviving examples, whether French, German, Italian, or Spanish, and including the Limoges and St. Gall groups, give the words a dramatic, ringing uplift, rl 1 ltd¹. As I have before mentioned, a few French versions prefer d r rl. Small variations of each version are to be found.

I now recall the claims of both Karl Young and Hardison that so many of the phrases of the *text* of the *Quem quaeritis* dialogue may well have been suggested by very similar phrases which occur in certain Easter liturgical pieces. I certainly agree. Various antiphon and responsory texts are set out by each author, familiar enough phrases appearing. Undoubtedly these acted as inspirations to the framer of the *Quem quaeritis* trope. Trope writers cast their nets wide over Vulgate and liturgy for textual material; many antiphons and responsories, also, were put to *incidental* use in both trope and *Visitatio* versions But for the *Quem quaeritis* dialogue setting *there was no borrowing of the music*. I have transcriptions of the musical settings of all the relevant liturgical pieces mentioned by both Karl Young and Hardison; they are all in the normal style of Gregorian chant. I can spare space for a setting down of no more than *three* of the most familiar of the antiphons (*vide* Young, 1, p. 203), from which, if the trope *had* sought a ceremonial origin, it might have drawn its music—but didn't.

From Carlsruhe, MS LX, fol. 93 (*thirteenth century*)

From Carlsruhe, MS LX, fol. 93r.

From Metz, MS 83, fol. 134.

Fig. 6. Although it is clear that the *Quem quaeritis* trope *text* may have gathered inspiration from antiphons such as these (derived at times from Vulgate sources), the *music* of the trope shows not the slightest links with the plainchant of such liturgical pieces.

It will be realized plainly enough that there is not the slightest musical link between these antiphons and the melody of the *Quem quaeritis* trope dialogue. I can say emphatically the same regarding the rest of the liturgical material referred to by the two authors, which I have also investigated. In any case, anyone really acquainted with the history of tropes and their actual character would realize the improbability that a trope—a free composition shaped for a specific purpose in a comparatively late period of Gregorian music —would have wanted, or would have had any need, to borrow anything from any ancient ceremonial music The basic style and temper of free trope-music belonged to its own, later age, however conciliatory it might be in small ways to the older composition to which it was attached, and which was the reason for its existence It may be useful to quote again briefly from that authority on the history of tropes and sequences, Jacques Handschin, concerning trope music:

...the music which was the foundation of this new art was already finding its way into the liturgy in the time of Amaldar (early 9th century) ...The new melodies are more vivid, less ornamental and sometimes remarkably impressive...Agobard, speaking of the danger that such music would swamp the liturgy, quotes passages from St. Jerome directed against "theatrical art".[18]

I offer one more illustration. Below is a transcription of the Introit of the Easter Mass itself, the music written in modern free-rhythm notation. Apart from the succeeding psalm verse (*"Domine probasti me ..."*), it consists of three sentences, interspersed by alleluias. Particularly to be noted are some of the alleluias, since I believe that certain small motives from them (*torculus* forms) were used by the trope composer to help to reconcile his more patterned music to the style of the parent piece. I feel supported by Willi Apel's words regarding Introit tropes in general, and the Introits with which they were associated, when he says (op. cit., p. 438): "the new music employs the same style (neumatic) the same range and tonality as the traditional chant, and occasionally even borrows a short motive from it."[19]

Fig. 7. This, the Introit proper of the Mass of Easter, is followed by a Psalm verse ("Domine probasti me...") and the *Gloria Patri*. The first part is then repeated.

Those readers who are sufficiently acquainted with Gregorian music might try singing, say, the St. Gall trope dialogue and follow it immediately by the "Resurrexi..." Introit. They will note the homogeneity of style, and in particular the setting of the words *"Quem quaeritis"* as compared with the music of the first, second and last of the Introit's alleluias. Some echoes are to be detected. I once more recall Handschin's words: "Every trope is in principle intended to combine with a given Gregorian song."

Altogether, it appears to me that the source of the *Quem quaeritis* trope was simply the *composer* of the *Quem quaeritis* trope, whoever he happened to be (I fear we shall never know). What I do feel sure about is that the trope couldn't have been lifted from some previous liturgical ceremony, especially not from one that has only a "theoretical" existence.

Can we at least guess the region of its origin? Jacques Chailley has no doubts. He says bluntly: "St. Martial de Limoges a inventé le trope *Quem queritis....*"[20] I think that the statement lacks absolute proof, but to me it seems very probable. The B.N. 1240 version, enclosed as it is within its own tropings, has the air of having been well established, and we can reasonably suppose that the trope's first, untrammelled appearance took place further back in time, in some yet undiscovered Limoges troper.

To my mind, the Limoges melodic shape is more spontaneous (more primitive, if you like) than the St. Gall version, which,

I believe, represents a later, more sophisticated shaping . The presence of the St. Gall "musical rhyme" and the somewhat more florid melodic line seems to support the view. If the *original* pattern had included the device of the musical rhyme at the two vocative phrases it seems unlikely to me that Limoges and other French versions, as well as the early Italians, would have abandoned it. *It does look as if the musical rhyme were an afterthought.* One small confirmation of this comes from a consideration of the so-called Dutch Easter Play, discovered a few years ago in the Royal Libary at the Hague. It consists of (A) a twelfth century manuscript lacking its first page, and (B) a fifteenth century and complete version. In both cases the music can be easily read. As for the *Quem quaeritis* dialogue, while the musical settings are in near agreement, the two vocative musical phrases of MS A *do not* rhyme; while MS B uses the same mnsic for "o coelicolae" as for "o Christicolae."

While on the subject of vocative phrases, I recall that I haven't explained how I dared stick in an "o" that wasn't there, before *"Christicolae"* in the St. Gall 484 version of the trope. Let us return to the St. Gall transcription, keeping an eye also on the photograph of the page of the manuscript.

I have read more than one book which makes a distinction between versions of the *Quem quaeritis* dialogue that have *"Christicolae"* with the "o," and *"Christicolae"* without the "o." The distinction is apparently taken seriously, one explanation offered being that *"Christicolae* without the 'o' "* was the original form, since the Angels were addressing mere mortals; while these latter in reply used the more respectful "o" form of address. Eventually, it was suggested, a sense of balance brought in the first-line "o." The explanation that the music brings is more mundane. It is that the "o" sound was there from the start—in performance. When it came to writing down something that was normally a matter of memory it sometimes got lost, owing to the fact that, practically, it formed what could easily amount to a continuous sound from the last syllable of "sepul-*chro.*" The best illustration I can give is to show extracts from a couple of eleventh century German twin versions, their dialogue music being very nearly that of St. Gall 484. These

are found in Berlin, Staatsbibl. MS lat. 4º 11, fol. 45v., and MS
lat. 4º 15, fol. 120. Copies of the relevant words and their St. Gall
neumes will be seen below (Fig. 8).

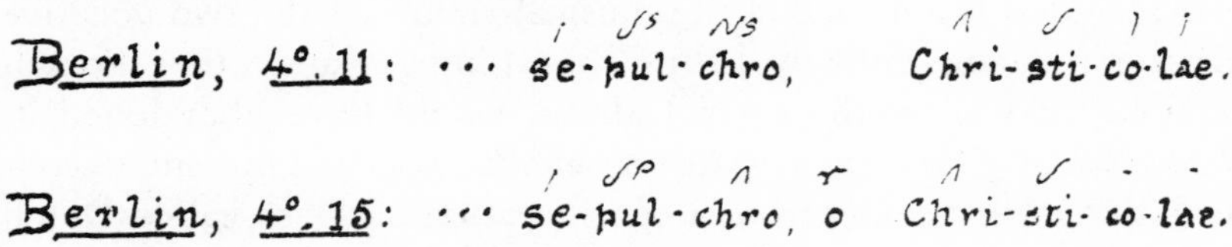

Berlin, 4º. 11: ··· se·pul·chro,   Chri·sti·co·lae.

Berlin, 4º. 15: ··· se·pul·chro, o Chri·sti· co·lae.

Fig. 8.

In the first case it can be seen that the "o" is missing, but over
the last syllable of "sepulchro" is a cluster of four note-units In
the second case the "o" is present, and two of the note-units have
been transferred across to supply its setting. In other words, in
performance the cases are the same. The music reading at "o"
in each case is, I believe, m– (a double note), and not rm (as in
MS 484). St. Gall versions of the tenth and eleventh centuries are
divided on this point.

I could give several more parallel instances (Apt 4 and Apt
X, for example)[21]. Here we have another case of musical clues
being the only evidence that could bring about a satisfactory
solution to a problem.

I will now turn to matters concerned with the famous Winchester
manuscripts, two documents which represent the earliest surviving
examples of *acted* "Quem quaeritis" dialogue. One of these is
contained in St. Ethelwold's *Regularis Concordia* (c. 970) which
from its rubrics gives us the earliest firm evidence as to how the
"Quem quaeritis" dialogue and some relevant following antiphons,
after their translation to the end of Matins, were used to produce a
truly dramatic version, a *Visitatio Sepulchri* prototype perhaps;
movements, gestures, tones of voice, elementary properties and
costuming all being detailed in the rubrics. The style is that of an
ordinarium, and thus the musical setting is absent, with the sung
words reduced to *incipits* (the usual *ordinarium* practice; vide Young 1,
p. 20). These *incipits* point to the same text as is found (with much
reduced rubrics) in the Winchester Troper version (which *has* its

music)—except that the second dismissal of the Marys, the antiphon, *Cito euntes . . .*, is omitted from the *Regularis* items. The two
versions seem more or less complementary, and one might reasonably assume that the *Regularis* "shorthand" version would have been
expanded readily enough when needed, into a normal *Visitatio*
performance, the music of which would be the "house" version for
Winchester, very much as set down in the *Troper*. But no; not
according to O.B. Hardison. He favours a theory, first advanced
by a German writer, J. Klapper, in a article written in 1932 on
The Origin of the Easter Play,[22] that there we have a *special type*, to be
accepted as it stands. Dealing with the *Visitatio* of the *Regularis
Concordia*, Hardison writes (p. 197).

. . . its dialogue is what will henceforth be called the "abbreviated form."
Instead of the familiar *Quem quaeritis in sepulchro, o Christocolae,* the rubrics
give only *Quem quaeritis,* and the Marys reply only *Ihesum Nazarenum.*
Editors have assumed that the dialogue is given as a series of *incipits,*
but the frequent recurrence of the abbreviated form in later manuscripts
suggests that the versions using it should be considered as a distinct type.
Since they have other features in common, they raise the possibility, first
suggested by Klapper, that the dialogue was originally an extremely
brief exchange of Biblical phrases supplemented by antiphons.[23]

In support of his claim Hardison directs us, in a footnote, to
eleven separate texts printed in Karl Young's first volume. The
separate types of these are as follows—one from a *missal,* five from
ordinariums, one from a *"directorium,"* and four from "unidentified
sources" mostly reproduced by Martène. When I take a look at
them I notice that Hardison has omitted to point out that all the
accompanying *liturgical* texts are similarly cut short, so that the
choir seemingly would sing, for example, "Ardens est"; "Quis
revolvet"; "Christus resurgens"; "Resurrexit Dominus"; and then,
after each pair of words, apparently dry up. Surely Hardison,
and others who have pursued this "abbreviated form" theory will
have realized the need, the *practical* reasons, for the use of *incipits*
in the type of service books such as the *ordinarium,* in which, for the
time being, the purpose is concentrated on rubrics and ceremonial
rather than texts and chant. Hardison invites us to seek further
for examples. I turn to my photographs, knowing that some

ordinariums are not so very strict as to the exclusion of music. Sure enough, I soon find such an example in a thirteenth century *ordinarium*, the details of which are Zurich, Zentralbibl., Ms Rheinau LIX, pp. 112-113. The *Quem quaeritis* dialogue is surrounded by various liturgical sentences, which are also given in *incipit* form. (Karl Young prints the text, op. cit., 1, pp. 596-7, completing the sentences throughout, but without following his usual practice of enclosing the added parts in pointed brackets since he is presenting it combined with another slightly varying version.) The *incipits* of the *Quem quaeritis* dialogue are: *"Que queritis"*; *"Ihm nazarenum"*; *"Non est hic"*; with the addition of *"Venite et videte locum"* (this last the start of an antiphon). All this is on the same lines as the quoted versions, but, as it happens, most of the liturgical *incipits* and *every syllable* of the "Quem quaeritis" dialogue *incipits* have their normal musical settings indicated. Must we think that these snatches of music got invented to accompany the original "abbreviated form," before the rest of the text and the rest of the setting got thought of —or is the most obvious answer the right one, i.e., that here we have a normal type, an *ordinarium*, in which, another liturgical purpose taking the leading place for the time being, texts and music are suffering a temporary cutting-down to brief but nevertheless unmistakable indications? I fear that the "abbreviated form" is yet another "textual" myth that must be abandoned.

In any case Hardison had already made one most unfortunate choice in the example that he culled from Karl Young (p. 262). For his argument he couldn't have chosen worse This version is of prime historical interest, a *Visitatio* performed in the most fitting place on earth, before the Holy Sepulchre itself in the Anastasis of the early twelfth century Jerusalem that had not long been captured by the Crusaders. The text is now preserved in Rome, Bibl. Vatic., MS Barberini lat. 649, Ordin. ad usum Hierosolymitanum anni 1160, fol. 75v.—76r. Its rubrics describe vividly the turbulent crowd of pilgrims who attended it. Karl Young has expanded the *incipits*, but, stretched to its full, the little music-drama would certainly have been on the brief side. However, the performance, according to Hardison, would have been briefer yet, amounting to just over a score of words, allowing for the first four to be sung three times, (*"cantando ter antiphonam"*), and might well have been over and done with before some of the turbulent pilgrims had settled in. I prefer to believe that the manuscript was in fact an *ordinarium*, and that Karl Young's version (plus the restored music) is likely to represent what was actually performed.[24]

Back to the Winchester *Regularis Concordia* (whose dramatic *Visitatio* is surely a normal *ordinarium*) and its *Winchester Troper* companion. Here is a striking fact which, as far as I am aware, nobody but myself has noted. The Anglo-Saxon neumes of the Winchester Troper dialogue indicate that it is very close to what might be called the "house" version of the St. Martial de Limoges troper group. There is one melodic peculiarity, which I shall presently detail, that links it uniquely with B.N. MS lat. 1240.

Considerations of space do not permit me to reproduce my version of the Winchester Troper *Visitatio Sepulchri*, in which I have set down the original Anglo-Saxon neumes together with my readings of them. The Bodleian Library at Oxford would readily supply photographs of the two pages of the Winchester Troper version, the details being, Oxford, Bibl. Bodl. MS 775 saec. x, fol. 17r.-17v. An eleventh century copy, the *Visitatio* confined conveniently to a single page, is to be found at Cambridge, Corpus Christi College, MS 473, fol. 26v.

Comparing the Limoges and Winchester versions, one notes that there are a few small differences in neume groupings that are inevitable when a version travelled. To name some of them—the "Winchester" setting of the first syllable of *"quae*ritis" fills the minor third gap of the *torculus* with a *quilisma*, that lightly-sung note which, as can be demonstrated, was frequently inserted at such a place whether or no the *quilisma* sign was written in. Winchester refuses Limoges' *quilisma* at "se*pul*chro" but has the descending liquescent which almost all of the St. Martial versions show. At *"o celicolae"* Winchester's setting is r͟m rd m͟f m r. So is that of B.N. M.S. lat. 1240; I will vouch for the fact that according to my charts nowhere in Christendom did any other *Quem quaeritis* dialogue version set the vocative phrase to those notes and that particular neume-grouping arrangement. The rest of the St. Martial tropers prefer rm rd m fm r or rm rd f mfm r. There is also the matter of the first vocative. As in the case of so many versions, the Winchester *Christicolae* is without its "o." The normal explanation is valid. Winchester's last syllable of "se-pul-*chro*" is given the neume group frrm; St. Martial de Limoges sets "–chro, o" to frrm.[25] It will be noted that Winchester ends its dialogue with the word *"dicentes"* (unlike St. Martial). I once constructed a chart of the music of all the dialogue versions from all over Christendom that used the *dicentes* ending, but could not find that it indicated any special linkings or had any other practical significance. The *Regularis* version, (without music) has instead *"a mortuis,"* which is unique, as far as I know, except for a late sixteenth century printed Italian version, which is much distorted musically.

The *Regularis Concordia* speaks of Winchester as having drawn a good deal on the monastic customs of Fleury and Ghent. Perhaps the Limoges music reached Winchester via Fleury, although there is no evidence as to any early dramatic activities at either Fleury or Ghent. Anyway, facts are facts. To me it seems more than likely that the dialogue music of the Winchester Troper came originally from St. Martial de Limoges.

A minor confirmation comes from the common presence at Limoges and Winchester of a very rare trope, which I give with its music:

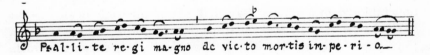

Psal-li-te re-gi ma-gno de vic-to mor-tis im-pe-ri-o.—

Fig. 9. This rare trope is found, uniquely, in B.N. 1240 as *prefacing* the *Quem quaeritis* trope. But it appears to have been used both at Limoges and Winchester (to the same music) as an *internal* trope of the Easter Introit "Resurrexi..."

In Karl Young's index it is put down as occurring only in B.N. MS lat. 1240, but it is to be found also in another Limoges troper, B.N. MS lat. 887. fol. 19r, and also on p. 19 of the Winchester Troper. Moreover, the music of all three is the same. Also, the *Regularis*, in the last rubric of its version of the drama, refers to the Prior as speaking of "rejoicing together at the triumph of our King, in that conquering Death, he arose," which is surely quite a good paraphrase of the *Psallite* trope.[26] The links between St. Martial de Limoges and Winchester as revealed by their music, seem pretty strong. (See my "Additional Note.")

I have in these pages applied the tests of musical evidence to but one single aspect of the medieval Church music-drama movement. To my mind, all parts of it are in need of a similar examination, and I am doing my best now to complete a book that does just that.

Karl Young has been blamed by some recent writers for having presented the "liturgical dramas" (I refrain from adding the qualifying "music-") in an "evolutionary" sequence of development, type by type, with scant respect for chronological considerations. There seem genuine grounds for this criticism. I believe, myself, that a much clearer appraisal of the historical situation is to be gained by setting out the identities of the surviving manuscripts, organized in their various types, in their chronological appearances. With some knowledge of the various individual contents, what evolutionary developments did in fact occur will then be more clearly apparent, especially when musical settings are allowed to bear witness. Were this to my immediate interest, I should have much to say concerning the dramatic and musical invention and construction which reached the pitch found in such little masterpieces of music-drama as the (so-called) "Fleury" *Visitatio Sepulchri*, the *Ordo ad representandum Herodem*, and the *Ordo Rachelis*.

I must question an opinion, voiced by Hardin Craig in his *English Religious Drama of the Middle Ages*, (Oxford, 1955). He deals in his early chapters with the "liturgical dramas," but (as usual) without paying the slightest attention to the musical evidence or, as far as I can tell, having sought the "feel" of the more substantial of these medieval Church works when they are given actual musico-dramatic performances. On p. 4 of his Introduction, he says that "the (*medieval*) religious drama had no dramatic technique or dramatic purpose, and no artistic self-consciousness.... " If this judgement is intended to apply to the best of the Church music-dramas, I am in the strongest disagreement. But this matter, at present, is not my business.[27]

I trust that in future, writers on the subject will bear in mind the century-old warning of Edouard de Coussemaker. The time is past when books can be written on the Church music-dramas propounding important theories based on the mere evidence of the libretti. The touchstone of the music must be brought to bear wherever possible. As it is, the music itself, time and again, reveals facts that textual study alone has failed to perceive.

NOTES

1. Karl Young, *The Drama of the Medieval Church*, 2 vols. (Oxford, 1933).

2. Oskar Schönemann, *Der Sündenfall und Marienklagen* (Hanover, 1855); Ferdinando Liuzzi, *La lauda e i primordi della melodia italiana*, 2 vols. (Rome, 1934), also his "L'espressione musicale nel dramma liturgico," *Studi Medievali*, 2 (1929), 74–109.

3. In the course of displaying the photographs of the musical examples at the Conference, I commented briefly on the types of musical notation to be seen: viz., (i) B.N. MS lat. 1240—roughly heighted Aquitaine neumes without any stave–lines: (ii) St. Gall MS 484—unheighted St. Gall type neumes without any stave lines [photographs of these first two dialogue examples can be seen on pp. 135 and 136 of this essay]; Modena, MS 0.1.7.—Italian neumes with note pitches almost exactly fixed, due to the use of a single horizontal clef-line marked as F, and some end-of-line "directs"; see p. 128 of this essay); (iv) Reims, MS 265—Metz-type neumes set on a four-line stave with C or F clefs, and B flats inserted where needed—pitch of notes completely certain; (v) B. de l'Arsenal, (Paris) MS 595—the Gregorian "square notation" has arrived—four-line stave with C or F clefs set down in absolute clarity; (vi) The Hague, Royal Library MS 71. J.70—an example of the ungainly German "horse-shoe-nail" notation—however, the identity of the notes quite clear.

4. De Coussemaker, Edouard, *Drames liturgiques du moyen âge* (Rennes, 1860), p. vi, vii, xii.

5. Regarding Gregorian neume notation, two standard and readily available works could be consulted: (a) Willi Apel's *Gregorian Chant* (Bloomington, 1958), pp. 99–132; (b) Gustave Reese's *Music in the Middle Ages* (New York, 1940), pp. 130–148. There is a useful chart that shows the main types of neume notation

in *Introduction à la Paléographie Musicale Grégorienne*, Planche C, by Dom Grégoire Suñol, O.S.B. (Paris, 1935).

6. The clarity of the setting of the "Maria Magdalena" *incipit* is not improved by the scribe having cancelled a spelling error in the line above by the simple means of an underlining—a series of dashes that intrude on the "Maria" neumes below. However, in my opinion the Rheinau neumes are closest to those found in Brit. Mus. MS lat. 23922 and Engelberg MS 314, both of which use the fourth text, given in full.

7. O.B. Hardison, Jr., *Christian Rite and Christian Drama in the Middle Ages* (Baltimore, 1965).

8. Ibid., pp. 189–90.

9. The "Resurrexit Dominus" referred to is no doubt *Alleluia, resurrexit Dominus hodie, resurrexit leo fortis, Christus filius Dei, Deo gratias, dicite eia!* The *Alleluia*, with a distinctive setting, is a constant feature of this trope.

10. Dom Grégoire Suñol, in that authoritative work of his, op. cit., p. 124, gives his opinion concerning medieval copyists in the following terms: "Autre constatation: nous pourrons nous rendre compte de la différénce de capacités intellectuelles chez les copistes. Si beaucoup sont cultivés, il s'en trouve aussi qui ne comprennent probablement ni le sens ni la signification de l'écriture, soit littéraire, soit surtout musicale, qu'ils transcrivent."

11. Edmund Martène, *De Antiquis Ecclesiae Ritibus*, 4 vols. (Venice, 1788).

12. In this monograph there has been disregarded an alternative *Quem quaeritis* dialogue exchange, later in date, with a new text and a new musical setting. It was a purely German novelty, first on record in a brief eleventh to twelfth century Easter music-drama, Einsiedeln MS 366, a unique version. In it, there is first the normal dialogue with its usual music, and then, (the idea being, apparently, that one could take one's choice) a dialogue that begins with *Quem quaeritis, o tremulae mulieres, in hoc tumulo plorantes?* The new setting is in the Phrygian mode, rather dull as compared with the earlier, vital music. Quite a number of later German *Visitatio* versions use the dialogue, with its music.

13. Jacques Chailley, *L'Ecole musicale de St. Martial de Limoges* (Paris, 1960).

14. The Aquitaine style of neume notation, which may have derived some of its features from that of Metz, developed a unique characteristic, the dissolving of the neumatic signs into single units, mostly "points," indicating individual pitches. See Apel, *op. cit.*, p. 120, for a brief comparative chart of the main neume styles. Also in the same work is a photograph of a page from Paris, B.N. MS lat. 776 of the eleventh century (Plate V). If the B.N. MS 1240 page represents Aquitaine notation at a low level, MS 776 is an example *par excellence*. The detached notes are accurately heighted round a scratched horizontal line (this not really visible in the reproduction), and altogether the melodies can be precisely read in regard to pitch. Those readers who consult the Apel book will find that seven of the eight Plates between pp. 122 and 123 reproduce various manuscript photographs of the text and music of the Easter Mass Introit, *Resurrexi, et*

adhuc tecum sum...One of them, Plate VIII, shows quite a different Introit setting, being an example of "Old Roman" chant, possibly pre-Gregorian.

15. Among St. Gall style neumes there is to be found the *episema* sign, a short stroke placed on top of a neume. It indicates the sustaining of something more than a normal note-length of sound, but whether this should mean a doubling or a less-fixed value is a matter for debate. The present transcriber wishes to take some note of these "lengthening" signs, but, using as he does a modern and somewhat informal notation, he finds himself compelled to employ doublings perforce.

16. Sol-fa notation should receive more serious attention than it seems to get at present from serious scholars of medieval music. After all, the idea of indicating the positions of tones and semitones in a diatonic scale by giving a distinctive name to each degree is as old as the ancient Greeks, and possibly older. The Benedictines of Solesmes make frequent use of sol-fa in their writings. It will be recalled that both Shakespeare and Samuel Pepys were well acquainted with the system, since their centuries inherited from medieval times the "hexachord" names—*ut, re, mi, fa, sol, la;* subsequently amended by the addition of the leading tone, *si,* and by *ut* being changed to the more vocal *do.* A modernization of the scale names has given us—*doh, ray, me, fah, soh, lah, ti (te), doh¹,* frequently simplified to d r m f s l t d¹. This last nomenclature is the labour-saving convention that will be used in this monograph for reproducing short musical examples. The attachment of more than one note to a single syllable will be indicated by underlinings, e.g., sd¹, fmr, mfsf, dl₁t₁dr. Attention is called to the use of upper and lower octave signs.

17. An error by Coussemaker in transcribing the *Quem quaeritis* dialogue music of Paris, B.N. MS lat. 1139 (he lacked the opportunities for wide comparisons) continues as the cover decoration to vol. 2 of E.K. Chambers' *The Medieval Stage,* 2 vols. (Oxford, 1903). To obtain a correct reading of the music of the phrase the B flat should be abolished, together with the C clef on the top staveline, and an F clef placed on the second line down. The phrase begins on D (2nd mode).

18. Jacques Handschin, "Trope, Sequence, Conductus," *Early Medieval Music up to 1300,* ed. A. Hughes, New Oxford History of Music, 2, (Oxford, 1954), p. 148.

19. Apel, op.cit., p. 438.

20. Chailley, op. cit., p. 373.

21. Apt "X" is a discovery of the present writer, not yet published. It has much in common with Apt 4 regarding the *Quem quaeritis* dialogue, but the music is in Aquitaine notation instead of Catalan.

22. J. Klapper, "Der Ursprung der lateinischen Osterfeiern," *Zeitschrift für deutsche Philologie,* 50 (1923), 46–58.

23. Hardison, op. cit., p. 197.

24. Viewing the little drama in more serious mood, and accepting the text as Karl Young expanded it, the present writer had no difficulty on one occasion in restoring the probable music, which would most likely to have been in the style of Northern France. The result was quite a "historical" acting-version.

25. In the course of reading his conference address the present writer put on view a comparative chart of the group of St. Martial *Quem quaeritis* tropes belonging to the tenth and early eleventh centuries. Undoubtedly there is a close "house" resemblance, even though the B.N. MS lat. 1240 version, so much earlier in date than the rest, chose to use as a concluding trope, *Alleluia, resurrexit Dominus hodie...*, while the other and later ones preferred, *Alleluia, ad sepulchrum residens...* and *En ecce completum....*

26. Professor Hardison, on p. 198, is in error when he says that "this verse, *with variations,*" (the present writer's italics) "is fairly common in manuscripts of the *Quem quaeritis.*" It isn't. He is perhaps referring to such tropes as *Psallite, fratres, hora est...* and *Hora est psallite...* These, however, are each of them completely independent compositions from *Psallite, regi magno...*, with quite different musical settings. A few examples only of these tropes have survived in *Quem quaeritis* use.

27. An example of the dangers of relying on second-hand texts without checking on ultimate sources can be seen in Hardin Craig's book, *English Religious Drama* (Oxford, 1955), pp. 37–38. He speaks of the "finished and original drama of Easter, a text from the Monastery of Saint Benoît-sur-Loire contained in the famous Fleury Playbook." (See Young, *op. cit.*, 1, pp. 393–97). He then goes on: "Another version of about the same degree of development from a thirteenth-century manuscript of Orleans in France is printed and translated by Adams." (See *Chief Pre-Shakespearean Dramas* by J. Quincy Adams [New York, 1924], pp. 15-20.) Again (p. 38) Craig speaks of "the Orleans version, like that in the Fleury Playbook..."

In point of fact, there are *not* two originals involved. The two printed versions mentioned represent one and the same text, and have but one single manuscript source, Orléans, Bibl. de la Ville MS 201, the "Playbook" version located on pp. 220–25.

Additional Note

W.H. Frere, in the Introduction to his well-known edition of the *Winchester Troper* (London, 1894), has called attention (p. xviii) to the large amount of "internal" troping of the Mass Introit which is to be found in tropers of the ninth century and onward for a while. Writers dealing with early versions of the *Quem quaeritis* trope usually end their text reproductions with the appearance of the Easter *Resurrexi, et adhuc tecum sum...* and seldom give any record of the *internal* tropes of the Introit which follow. If these are investigated it will be found that the identity of these compositions varied a good deal from center to center, and at times (with their musical settings) offer useful information as do, of course, the various additional sentences that link the *Quem quaeritis* to the beginning of the Easter Introit. Thus, while the St. Martial B.N. MS lat. 1240 has for its linking trope, *Alleluia, resurrexit Dominus hodie*...and follows the first sentence of the Introit (*Resurrexi*...) with the "internal" trope, *Dormiui pater exurgam diluculo, et somnus meus dulcis est mihi: (Posuisti*...), the later St. Martial tropers use for links two sentences, *Ad sepulchrum residens*... and *En ecce completum*, ..., and begin the internal troping of the Introit not with *Dormiui*...but with such a sentence as *Ecce pater cunctis ut iusserat*...Similar varities of regional choice are found in German, Italian and other French groups. It is therefore significant when we discover that the first internal tropings of the Easter Introit as found in the St. Martial B.N. MS lat. 1240, 30 v., (*Dormiui pater exurgam diluculo*...; *Ita pater, sic placuit ante te, u moriendo*...; and *Qui abscondisti haec sapientibus*...) are exactly paralleled, music and all, at the corresponding places in the Winchester Troper (fo. 19v.). Moreover, later tropings (of a repeat of the Introit) show further correspondences, even though the order of the sentences is sometimes changed. Here surely is another piece of evidence that suggests close links between St. Martial de Limoges and Winchester.